A

THEOLOGY

FOR THE

NEW

MILLENNIUM

The Cathedral of the Holy Spirit
4650 Flat Shoals Parkway
Decatur, GA 30034

Tel: (404) 243-5020 Fax: (404) 243-5927
(WEBSITE) http://www.earlpaulk.com
(E-MAIL) cathedral@randomc.com

INTRODUCTION

If one has a true revelation from God, it becomes an absolute to leave it for posterity. The church of today is indebted to church fathers for leaving us a record of God's insight for revelation given to them. God has never given His complete revelation to any one person which makes us dependent on many for God's message to man. After diligently studying the Word of God and systematic theology penned by the "greats", I was able to add my Pentecostal flavor and write a very simple book, "Your Pentecostal Neighbor" in my early ministry. I was content for many years and then became desperately hungry to know more.

As a young pastor, I inquired of my Dad, who was an outstanding Pentecostal preacher, about the Kingdom God. His response was that the kingdom age was reserved for a future millennium. My trust was so complete in him that I sought the matter no further. The closest I came to receiving insight on the Kingdom of God was while in seminary at Candler School of Theology, Emory University. E. Stanley Jones came to the campus to preach. I did not attend his services, and was to learn in later years that he had great revelation on the Kingdom of God.

Then on one Saturday night I had a tremendous visitation from God and was given revelation on the Kingdom of God. My life was changed and my preaching and practices changed forever. My pastorate became a demonstration of the kingdom principles.

God put among us at the Cathedral a very studious young minister just out of seminary. Dan Rhodes became a pastor on the staff and was with us when God favored me with the message on the Kingdom of God. With his own Biblical insight, he began making notes on the messages and teachings that God was granting us at the Cathedral. He has now released his work after a number of years. He desired no recognition, but it is expedient for the reader to know that without his work, the message that God has given me would never be put together in this fashion.

Both Dan and I are very desirous that the message of this thesis live on and on. You will find sound incarnational theology with new insight on the Kingdom of God. As you study the following pages, we pray that God will use it to hasten the day when a mature church can receive the return of the Bridegroom, our Lord, Jesus Christ.

Earl Paulk, Th. D., D. D.
Archbishop

PREFACE

THE CATHEDRAL OF THE HOLY SPIRIT AT CHAPEL HILL is *"Orthodox"* in our theology drawing from the theological foundations provided by Polycarp, Ignatius, Tertullian, Cyprian Augustine and other Apostolic and Early Church Fathers. We embrace without reservation the great creeds of the historic Christian Church to include the Apostles Creed of 390 AD, the Nicene Creed of 325 AD, the Athenasian Creed of the early 5hcentury, and the statement of Chaledon of 451 AD. The Cathedral of the Holy Spirit is *"Reformed"* in our doctrine accepting the great theological reforms of the 16th and 17th century through Luther, Calvin, Zwingli and the Puritan writers. The Cathedral of the Holy Spirit is *"Catholic"* in our immovable conviction that the Church of the Lord Jesus Christ throughout the world is one Holy and Apostolic Church being "one body with one Spirit, one Lord and one faith". Consequently, all Christian leaders and churches have a common purpose to work cooperatively and collectively to reach the world for Christ. The Cathedral of the Holy Spirit is *"Evangelical"* in our doctrinal adherence to the authority of Scripture, the deity of Christ, and salvation through faith in the atoning work of Christ. The Cathedral of the Holy Spirit is *"Charismatic"* in our worship and ministry, partaking of the power of the Holy Spirit and exercising the biblical gifts which are given to the Church. Through the empowering work of the Holy Spirit, we zealously reach out to our community and the world by demonstrating the compassion of Christ and offering His Gospel of salvation, hope and restoration. The Cathedral of the Holy Spirit is *"Christological"* in our belief that the Lord Jesus Christ is central in our worship and Christian practices. We proclaim Jesus to be the Lord of our lives, the Head of His Church and the King of His kingdom. The Cathedral of the Holy Spirit is *"Incarnational"* in our theology, not that we are Christ, but that Christ is in us and we are in the world reaching the lost, continuing His work and demonstrating His kingdom on earth. The Cathedral of the Holy Spirit is *"Covenantal"* in our theology believing that full partnership with God in accomplishing His purposes on earth is possible only through our response to His covenant. God's covenant with His people is dramatized in the Old Testament through human experience and is fully ratified in the New Testament through the atoning work of Christ. The Cathedral of the Holy Spirit is *"Restorational"* in our practical theology knowing that the central work of God as recorded in both the Old and New Testament is restoring man, the earth, and the universe from the corruption of evil back to God's original plan and purpose. The Cathedral of the Holy Spirit is *"Kingdom"* in our theology believing that the central issue and concern of God in Scripture is His righteous rule in heaven and on earth. Since the Kingdom of God was the major subject preached and taught by Christ during His earthly ministry and after His resurrection, the Church, therefore, is the embassy of the Kingdom of God on earth and must proclaim Christ as both Savior and Lord of all.

THE MINISTRY OF THE CATHEDRAL OF THE HOLY SPIRIT expresses the following theological statement of foundational Christian truths, based upon the Bible, which is our all-sufficient written rule for faith and practice. *This statement is not an attempt to disprove others in their personal views of scripture or to be a point of argument or debate.* This statement is, however, intended both as a basis of fellowship among us that we all speak the same things concerning our faith [1] and that we should know the purposes of God on the earth and how we as a local church should focus our energies to become an instrument of God to accomplish His Will.[2] No claim is made that it contains all biblical truth, only that it covers our need as to these foundational doctrines. We do not presume to say the phraseology employed in this Statement is a substitute for Scripture or that it is the final work on Bible truth. We are, however, persuaded that it is proper and consistent with the Holy Scripture to "set forth in order a declaration of those things which are most surely believed among us.[3]

1-(1 Cor. 1: 10; Acts 2:42); 2-(Phil. 2:13-15; Heb. 13:20-21); 3-(Luke 1: 1-3).

ACKNOWLEDGMENTS

The vast majority of this Theological Statement, most specifically the concepts of the Kingdom of God and the role of the Church, are direct products of the ministry and teaching of Archbishop Earl Paulk. In addition, we are indebted to the great theologians of the past and those of the present who have influenced and formulated the basic theological premises of the Christian Faith and who have established a proven order of theological thought. Among those whom we specifically acknowledge and from whom we have drawn theological insights are the works of Louis Berkhof, "Systematic Theology"; Millard J. Erickson, "Christian Theology"; J. Rodman Williams, "Renewal Theology"; and the lectures and teachings of Ern Baxter.

To Pastor Clariece Paulk, we are appreciative for her expertise in proofing and editing the initial manuscript.

For tireless work and countless hours of formatting this document for presentation, we give thanks to Charlotte Lemons and other staff members who helped to coordinate this project.

To Wendy Long, we give a special word of gratitude for the hours it took to make the final grammatical corrections and edits to this revised manuscript.

For the input of sound Biblical teaching and preaching that has added depth to many of these theological concepts, we give special thanks to the ministries of the Presbytery of the Cathedral of Chapel Hill.

Finally, we thank Nolan McCants - Cover Design Concepts & Coordinator and Paul Phillips - Graphic Illustrator.

Contents

I. THE BIBLE

A. Of its Origin

The Bible is the written revelation of God concerning Himself, His Word and His eternal purposes. It reveals to us the intention of His heart and mind toward all people, nations and even the whole of creation itself. Though God used human instruments to write the original manuscripts of the Bible, it, nevertheless, originated from heaven [1] being inspired (or in-breathed) by God Himself and is in fact the very "Word of God". [2] Both the Old and New Testaments constitute the written canon of Scripture which we consider to be the holy writ of God. Only through the power of the Holy Spirit can the minds of men and women be opened [3] to understand that Scripture is the Word of God [4] and that it is relevant and applicable to all generations. When enlightened by the Holy Spirit, the Bible is able to be understood as the all-sufficient, infallible rule of faith and conduct and is the guide to salvation, worship and service unto God. [5]

1-(John 1:1-5, 14; Ps. 119:89); 2-(2 Tim. 3:15-17; 2 Pet. 1:20-21); 3-(John 16:13-15; Luke 24:45); 4-(1 Thess. 2:13); 5-(2 Tim. 3:15-17; 1 Pet. 1:23-25).

B. Of its Authority and Power

The Bible is the "Testament" or Covenant of God extended to all people. For those who are obedient, it carries the fully ratified authority of God to bring to pass all the Covenantal promises written in Scripture. Even as the "spoken" Word of God is His power by which He both created and sustains His universe, [1] so also the "written" Word of

God is His sacramental power by which He brings and sustains salvation to all who have united their faith with His Word. [2] Through willing obedience and trust in God's Word, believers are given the authority and power of God to act on His behalf, [3] withstand sin, [4] war against and overcome the devil, [5] fulfill God's purposes [6] and inherit the promises and blessings written in Scripture.[7]

1-(Gen. 1:1-31; Heb. 1:3); 2-(Rom. 1:16; 1 Cor. 1:18; Heb. 4:1-2); 3-(Exodus 19:5-6; John 8:31); 4-(Psalm 119:11); 5-(Eph. 6:12-17; Matt. 4:3-11; Rev. 12:11); 6-(Eph. 2:10; 2 Tim. 1:9); 7-(1 Kings 2:3-4; Eph. 1:11; 2 Pet.1: 4).

C. Of its Purpose and Content

God gave the Bible to reveal Himself to man and to show how He restores His rule to a universe that has been disrupted by rebellion. Specifically, the Bible is God's written standard that reveals His true character, [1] the person of Christ, [2] the work of the Holy Spirit, [3] the wicked schemes and plans of Satan, [4] and the purpose and plight of man. [5] The Bible also makes known the redemptive work of God that restores man to his original purpose, [6] and it discloses God's intentions for the Church [7] to influence the world with His rule (His Kingdom). [8] It is by his standard that human plans, motives, actions and words are judged. [9] It is by this standard working through the Church that all powers and principalities in heaven and earth are ultimately accountable [10.] The Word of God accurately understood by the power of the Holy Spirit becomes the wisdom and counsel of God for His people to fulfill their purpose on the earth.[11] For this reason an intimate working knowledge of God's Word is an absolute necessity for every Christian believer. [12]

1-(1 John 4:16;); 2-(Matt. 16:16-17; John 20:31); 3-(John 14:16-17; Acts 1:8); 4-(John 10:10; Eph. 6:11-12); 5-(Gen. 1:26-28; Rev. 12:9-11); 6-(Eph. 1:4-11); 7-(Matt. 16:18-19); 8-(Acts 1:8; Rev, 11:15); 9-(Heb. 4:12-13); 10-(I Cor. 6:2-3; Eph. 3:10); 11-(2 Tim. 3:15-17); 12-(Ps. 119:9, 11, 97-105; 2 Tim. 2:15).

II. GOD

A. Of His Existence and Ability to be Known

According to the biblical record, there is never a question whether or not God exists. Rather it explicitly states who He is, what He does and how He deals with people. There is one and only one [1] true and living [2] God who is a self-existent, [3] self-conscious, [4] personal Being, [5] who purposefully created and rules the universe [6] and who is able to be known only by His self-revelation.[7] Because God's infinite Being is totally beyond human comprehension, He makes Himself known through the evidence of His creation,[8] the Holy Scriptures,[9] the conviction of the believer's faith, [10] and the testimony of the Holy Spirit living in the heart of the believer.[11] The ultimate and most accurate self-revelation of God is His Son, Jesus Christ, who is the exact representation of God's character and nature [12] lived out through a real human being without the stain of sin. [13]

1-(Deut. 6:4; 1 Cor. 8:4-6); 2-(Jer. 10:10; I Thess. 1:9); 3-(Ex. 3:14; John 5:26) 4-(Jer. 29:11; Hosea 11:8); 5-(Ex. 19:4-6; Rev. 3:20) 6-(Ps. 103:19; Rev. 4:11); 7-(1 Chr. 28:9; Matt. 11:25-27; John 6:44); 8-(Rom. 1:19-20); 9-(Luke 24:25-27; John 5:39); 10-(Heb. 11:1, 6); 11-(1 John 5:7, 10); 12-(John 14:8-11; Heb. 1:1-3); 13-(John 1:1, 14; Heb. 4:15).

B. Of His Identity

God is *Living*. He has life in Himself, [1] gives life and breath to all things, [2] and is alive today.[3] God is not an impersonal force in nature or the universe, [4] but He is a *Personal*, caring Being [5] who seeks out fellowship with man [6] and graciously initiates and enters into a covenant relationship with him.[7] God is *Spirit*. [8] He is not flesh and blood, but is invisible, [9] existing as total dynamic and totally free and uncoerced to do as He wills.[10] Because of the infinite and eternal dimension of God's Being, His identity cannot be separated from His attributes. Hence, God does not merely *have* love, goodness, holiness, justice, wisdom, truth and power, but more accurately, God *is* love, goodness, holiness, justice, wisdom, truth and power. By virtue of His absolute deity and the eternal greatness of His Being, the works of creation glorify God and He alone is worthy to be worshipped and served by all moral creatures.[11]

1-(John 5:26); 2-(Gen. 2:7; John 1:3); 3-(Heb. 7:25; 13:8); 4-(Rom. 1:20-23); 5-(Ezek. 34:11; John 3:16); 6-(Rev. 3:20); 7-(Ex. 6:4-7); 8-(John 4:24); 9-(1 Tim. 6:16); 10-(Jer. 32:27); 11-(Ps. 103:20-22; Ps. 145:10; Ex. 20:3-6).

C. Of His Transcendence

God transcends all that we as humans see, hear, taste, smell or feel. God is *Infinite* in His Being and nature and is therefore unlimited and unrestricted in all that He is.[1] Since His realm of existence is infinitely beyond the finite limitation of spatial creation, [2] our only proper response to Him is genuine reverence, humility and obedience.[3] God is *Eternal*. He is the only reality without beginning or end.[4] He both created and transcends time and space, thus He freely moves in and out of His creation at will.[5] God is *Unchanging*. [6] He is totally dependable and consistent in His character, acts and purposes.

1-(Job 11:7-10); 2-(Is. 55:8-9); 3-(Ex. 34:6-8); 4-(Ps. 90:2; 1 Tim. 1:17); 5-(Matt. 17:2-8; Luke 24:29-31); 6-(Mal. 3:6; Heb. 6:17; James 1:17).

D. Of the Mystery of the Godhead

The total understanding of God's Trinitarian existence is infinitely beyond our comprehension as finite human beings. While God is one undivided divine Essence, [1] He is also a complex manifold Being in which there are three persons [2] (separate, rational, moral identities). To each Person of the Trinity belongs the undivided essence and full attributes of God such that the *Father is God*; [3] the *Son is God*; [4] and the *Holy Spirit is God*. [5] Each Person of the Trinity is distinct; each eternally existed prior to creation, [6] and each has specific external acts in regard to creation and redemption. The Father is the Originator and Creator of all things. [7] The Son is the Instrument through which the Father created all things and is the Executor of redemption, becoming incarnate for the purpose of the atonement. [8] The Holy Spirit was also involved in the creation process and is now the active Empowerment of God on earth applying the atoning work of Christ to the hearts of believers and enabling men to believe and serve God. [9] The belief in the Trinity is absolutely essential to Christian doctrine since if the Trinity does not exist, then neither does the Son of God or the Holy Spirit. Consequently, the redemptive work of the Son and the Holy Spirit would not exist. Salvation would not be available to men, and they would remain eternally lost in their sins.[10]

1-(Deut. 6:4; Mark 12:29); 2-(Gen. 1:26; Matt. 28:19); 3-(Matt. 6:9); 4-(John 10:30; Col. 2:9); 5-(John 15:26); 6-(John 15:26; 17:5); 7-(Gen. 1:1; John 7:33; 14:26, 28); 8-(Col. 1:12-17; John 1:1-3, 14); 9-(Gen. 1:2; Job 33:4; John 16:13-14; Acts 1:8); 10-(1 Cor. 15:12-19; John 3:5-8).

E. Of His Character

Since the attributes of God are inseparable from His eternal Being, when Scripture states that God is love, it naturally follows that God's character must also be **Love.**[1] God's love is never self-seeking but forever self-giving and patient toward the plight of human kind.[2] The love of God is unconditional toward man, meaning that human merit cannot earn His love and neither will any action on the part of man cause God to withdraw His love.[3] A human expression of God's infinite love is found in 1 Cor. 13:4-7. It is this type of love that becomes the motivating force for His grace, mercy, kindness, and goodness toward man.[4] In addition to love, God's character is also infinite in **Holiness,** [5] meaning that divine moral purity is at the very foundation of His being. His holiness is expressed as righteousness,[6] and His righteous acts are always just and impartial.[7] In the holiness of His character, God will never allow sin to remain unpunished, but will bring effectual correction to all injustice and inequity in the universe in the fullness of time.[8] Therefore, God must never be considered the author of evil, but in fact, He overcomes evil with good even to the extent of reversing its effects.[9] Furthermore, the infinite character of God is **Truth,** [10] meaning that there is no deception or falsehood in Him.[11] The outward acts of God are completely faithful [12] and consistent with His internal character. Thus, God will never forsake nor break covenant once He establishes it.[13] The conclusion, therefore, is that God's unfathomable Being and character is infinite in **love, grace and mercy; _and at the same time_**, He is equally infinite in **holiness, righteousness and justice**. It is essential to comprehend that, unlike our human nature, there are no opposing forces within

God's character. The Lord is neither frustrated nor torn between His love for fallen man and His justice that deals righteously with sin. Thus, the fullness of these amazing attributes all meet in the eternal greatness of our God and Savior.[14]

1-(1 John 4:8); 2-(John 3:16; Rom 5:8); 3-(Deut. 7:7-8; John 15:16); 4-(Ex. 34:6; Ps. 23:6; 100:5); 5-(Is. 6:3; Rev. 4:8); 6-(Ps. 25:8; Rev. 15:4); 7-(Ps. 89:14; Rom. 2:11); 8-(Ex. 34:7; 2 Pet. 2:9; 3:7-13); 9-(Hab. 1:13; 1 John 3:5; Gen. 50:20; Rom. 12:21); 10-(John 14:6); 11-(Heb. 6:18); 12-(Deut. 32:4); 13-(Gen. 9:9-16; Rom. 3:3; Heb. 13:5; 2 Tim. 2:13); 15-(Ps. 85:9-10).

F. Of the Great Sovereign Power of God

God is the almighty,[1] **all-powerful** (omnipotent) God, who has absolute energy to accomplish whatsoever He wills and to implement all His eternal purposes.[2] God, in His unlimited power,[3] not only created all things, but also sustains[4] and directs all life toward His divine purposes.[5] Consequently, there is no obstacle outside God that can thwart His free expression.[6] God is **all-knowing** and all-wise (omniscient),[7] meaning that He is able to view the past, present and future with equal clarity.[8] There is no creature hidden from His sight and He knows the thoughts and intentions of every heart.[9] God is **all-present** (omnipresent) in the entirety of His creation.[10] The transcendence of God over the limitations of the time/space world is far greater than mere spatial orientation since God is immediately present and available to every person everywhere in both heaven and earth at the same time.[11] Yet within His sovereign rule, God has also made provision for the freedom of man's will to fully operate with inherent consequences or rewards related to his personal choices and decisions.[12] Nevertheless, in the great sovereign fore-knowledge of God, He reserves the right to allow the consequences of wrong choices to remain or to alter the outcome of the choices in order that His higher eternal purposes may be accomplished.[13]

1-(Gen. 17:1; Rev. 4:8); 2-(Is. 46:9-11); 3-(Jer. 32:17, 27); 4-(Col. 1:16-17; Heb. 1:3); 5-(Rom. 8:28); 6-(Job 42:2; Is 43:13); 7-(Ps. 147:5; Rom. 11:33; 16:27); 8-(Is. 46:10); 9-(Heb. 4:12-13); 10-(Ps. 139:7-10); 11-(Jer. 23:23-24; Matt. 28:20); 12-(Deut. 30:15-20; Is. 1:18-20); 13-(Gen. 50:20; Prov. 21:1; Rom. 8:28; 1 Tim. 1:15-16).

G. Of the Eternal Purposes and Plan of God for Heaven and Earth

God, whose eternal plan for the universe was established before the foundations of the earth[1], foreknows in His omniscience all future events in heaven and on earth, both good and evil. Accordingly, in order to bring forth His eternal plan and guarantee it's success regardless of human opposition, God strategically sets in place *certain predetermined decrees and laws that most assuredly will bring His will to pass*.[2] Even though it is impossible for the human mind to fully comprehend the mystery of God's will, what God has revealed must be declared[3] and understood by the Church if she is to become God's instrument through which He fulfills His will on earth. God's eternal purposes become evident through the study of His Word, His decrees, His promises, His acts, and the declarations of His will. The following decrees, which God has purposed, become essential elements of His eternal plan for both heaven and earth.

1-(Ps. 33:11; Is. 46:9-11; Matt. 25:34); 2-(2 Chr. 20:6; Is. 14:27); 3-(Deut. 29:29; Acts 20:27; 1 Cor. 2:9-10; Eph. 1:9-11; Rev. 1:11, 19).

1. God has purposed that *HIS AUTHORITY* is and will be forever preeminent.

God is the ultimate authority in the universe [1] and all creation belongs to Him by virtue of His creative acts. God has decreed that every moral creature (whether in heaven or on earth) will ultimately bow to His righteous rule. God blesses and rewards those who willingly obey with humble and submitted hearts; however, those who rebel against His authority will experience the full weight of His dominion in judgment. [2] All other authorities (whether angelic or human) do not have inherent authority but are delegated by God for the purpose of representing His righteous will. Through the principle of willing submission to His authority, God is glorified in such a way that His knowledge and glory will most certainly fill all the earth and His righteous rule will be manifested forever. [3] If the world is going to see a demonstration of God's glory and His Kingdom (His righteous rule) on the earth, then the Church must be unified in her mission. She must be obedient to God's preeminent authority, and become faithful vessels that express the light and fragrance of His presence on earth.[4]

1-(Is. 43:12-13; 45:22-23; 46:9-11); 2-(Is. 45:23-24; Luke 20:17-18; Phil. 2:10-11; 1 Pet. 5:6; Rev. 19:15); 3-(Num. 14:20-23; Is. 11:9; 2 Pet. 3:13; Rev. 11:15); 4-(Is. 60:1-3; John 17:21-23; 2 Cor. 2:14-15; 3:18; Rom. 1:8; 16:19; Col. 1:26-28).

2. God has purposed to manifest the drama of His eternal plan in the *VISIBLE CREATION*

The world that is seen is God's visible creation of time and space suspended in the invisible world of eternity. Since all things were created by Him and for His purposes, the world serves as God's "stage" (or arena) where He sovereignly manifests the unfolding drama of His plan, carries out His eternal decrees, and brings the righteous rule of His heavenly Kingdom to the earth.[1] Consequently, there is an interaction between these two worlds such that the visible creation is a recipient of the drama of events that occurred and continue to occur in the invisible realm of heaven.[2] Likewise, events on earth are witnessed by and affect the heavenly world.[3] Thus, God has purposed that through the obedient actions of His Church on earth, He will establish His witness against the rebellion that disrupted the invisible realm of heaven.[4] Therefore, if the Church is going to fulfill the will of God, she must visibly demonstrate His rule and His character before all authorities both in heaven and on earth.[5]

1-(Matt. 6:10; Col. 1:16-17; Rev. 4:11; 11:15); 2-(Rom. 1:19-23; 8:19-22; Rev. 12:3-10); 3-(Heb. 11:39-40; 12:1; Luke 15:7; Rev. 6:9-11); 4-(Job 1:6-12,20-22; Rom. 12:19-21; 2 Cor. 10:3-6; Eph. 6:12-13; Rev. 12:11); 5-(1 Cor. 11:10; Eph. 3:9-11; 1 Pet. 2:18-23).

3. God has purposed to prepare *A PEOPLE FOR HIS OWN POSSESSION.*

God is a personal and loving God who willingly offers to share Himself with all His moral creatures. With great patience and merciful acts, God graciously invites all men, in spite of their rebellious bent, to be included in His eternal plan and to enter into a personal relationship with Him.[1] Those who respond in covenant to the redemptive work of Christ with grateful and obedient hearts become "the People of God".[2] Through the sanctifying work of the Holy Spirit, God continues to mature and prepare His people to be His witness and demonstration of the Kingdom of God on the earth.[3] Accordingly, if the Church is going to fulfill the will of God on earth, she must yield to the transforming work of the Holy Spirit and become that people which God has prepared for His special purpose.[4] And this is the witness that God gives to the world: A unified Church, in oneness with each other and with Christ, through whom God shows Himself strong.[5]

1-(1 Sam. 12:22; Is. 65:1-2; Mal. 3:17-18; Titus 2:14); 2-(John 1:11-13; 1 Pet. 2:9-10); 3-(Ex. 19:4-6; Deut. 30:9-10; Luke 8:15; 1 Peter 2:9-10); 4-(Luke 1:17; Rom. 8:28-30; 12:1-2; 2 Cor. 3:18); 5-(John 17:21-23; 2 Chr. 16:9; Eph. 3:16-21).

4. God has purposed to give *FREEDOM OF CHOICE* to all His moral creatures.

God created all His moral creatures with the freedom to obey Him or to defy His rule. This Biblical truth is clearly demonstrated by the direct commands and options that God sets before His people.[1] God established the power of choice in His universe as a point of testing to determine levels of loyalty and devotion to Him and His cause. Through freedom of choice, the angels were allowed to choose between maintaining their assigned place of authority or transgressing the command of God.[2] Through freedom of choice, God examines the hearts of men and women in order to find those who have fully given themselves to Him.[3] If we, as God's Church, will learn that the power of choice is a determining principle in God's eternal plan, then we will be able to guard our hearts from evil and make obedient choices that glorify Him and confirm us to be His people.[4]

1-(Gen. 2:9, 16-17; 3:6-7; Deut. 30:15-20; John 3:16, 36); 2-(Is. 14:12-15; 2 Pet. 2:4; Jude 6); 3-(Deut. 8:1-20; 2 Chr. 16:9; 1 Pet. 1:6-9); 4-(Prov. 4:23-27; Matt. 21:28-31; John 13:34-35; 15:8-10).

5. God has purposed that all creation will ultimately be *ACCOUNTABLE* to Him.

God has made it unmistakably clear that He will bring every living creature to a place of personal accountability for what is done or not done.[1] God applies the principle of accountability without partiality to all creation including the angelic world, [2] nations and cities of the earth, [3] leaders of God's people, [4] the Church, [5] every human being whether godly or ungodly [6] and even the animal and plant world.[7] God's plan for accountability includes rewards for obedience and punishments for rebellion, which affects not only this life but also the life to come. [8] Therefore, since accountability is inevitable, we as Christians must be diligent and faithful in our individual obedience to God. [9] Likewise, God's Church in its corporate accountability must be obedient to Christ's great commission to reach all the world with the Gospel of Christ and the demonstration of His Kingdom.[10]

1-(Eccles. 12:13-14; Rom. 14:11-12; James 4:17); 2-(2 Pet. 2:4; Jude 6; Rev. 12:7-9; 20:1-3, 10); 3-(Ps. 2:1-12; Matt. 11:20-24); 4-(Matt. 23:11-35; James 3:1; Heb. 13:17); 5-(1 Pet. 4:17; Rev. 3:1, 14-16); 6-(Ps. 50:4-6; John 5:28-29; Rev. 20:12-13); 7-(Ex. 21:28-32; Mark 11:13-14, 20-21); 8-(Deut. 28:1-68; Luke 18:28-

30; Rom. 2:5-11; Gal. 6:7-8); 9-(Rom. 14:11-12; 2 Cor. 5:10); 10-(Matt. 24:14; 28:19-20; Mark 16:15).

6. God has purposed to establish *HIS COVENANT* through which He relates to fallen man and restores all that has been corrupted.

God, in His infinite mercy and unfathomable foreknowledge, has established His eternal Covenant[1] (which predates both man and creation) as a "spiritual bridge" over which God reaches and restores fallen man. In keeping with God's purposes, His Covenant is the only provision by which man can be delivered from evil, [2] forgiven of sins [3] and restored to his original purpose. [4] In addition, God extended His Covenant to include the eventual restoration of the earth and all living creatures that have been corrupted by sin.[5] Even though God makes full provision for restoration, it is nevertheless conditional upon man's response. [6] When man responds in faith and obedience to God's promises, meets the conditions of the Covenant and faithfully endures the testing of his Covenant,[7] he is restored to a divine partnership with God to accomplish His eternal purposes on earth. Through the provision of Covenant, God gives providential care and ultimate victory even in the most difficult of circumstances.[8] Because of the essential nature of Covenant in the Christian's life, the Church must be diligent to understand and accurately teach people how to respond to and enter into this gracious provision of God.

1-(Ps. 111:9; Heb. 13:20); 2-(Gen. 6:17-18; Ex. 6:5-7); 3-(Ex. 24:7-8; Matt. 26:26-28; Heb. 9:11-15); 4-(Zech. 9:11-12; Jer. 29:11-14; Acts 3:19-21); 5-(Gen. 9:9-17; 2 Pet. 3:12); 6-(Ex. 19:5-

6; Lev. 26:14-18); 7-(Deut. 8:2; James 1:2); 8-(Gen. 22:17-18; Ex. 6:5-7; 2 Chr. 21:7; Ps. 121:1-8).

7. God's ultimate purpose is to *CORRECT AND RESTORE* a universe in rebellion.

Corruption and chaos entered God's once peaceful and harmonious universe[1] through rebellion and sin from both the angelic and the human worlds.[2] Out of God's foreknowledge of these tragic events, He decreed (before they ever happened) that He would ultimately destroy the curse of evil and restore all things back to the glory of their original condition under the order and control of His righteous rule.[3] Since it was through Satan that man was corrupted, God in His infinite wisdom and justice has chosen to ultimately defeat the devil by the witness of his own victim.[4] If the Church, as recipients of God's grace and restoration, is going to fulfill His will on earth, then she must become His instrument through which God can overcome the devil and restore what he has destroyed.[5] By overcoming evil with good and restoring people who are trapped in sin, the Church demonstrates God's gracious work of restoration and brings glory to Him forever.[6]

1-(Job 38:7; Is. 45:18; Ezek. 28:12-14); 2-(Gen. 1:2; Ezek. 28:15-17; Rev. 12:7-9; Rom. 5:12); 3-(Num. 14:21; Rom. 14:11; 2 Pet. 3:13; Rev. 22:3); 4-(Luke 10:17-19; Eph. 3:10; Rom. 16:20); 5-(1 Tim. 1:13-16; 1 John 3:8; Rev. 12:11;); 6-(Rom. 12:17-21; Gal. 6:1; Heb. 13:20-21).

III. CREATION AND MAN

A. Of Creation

God's original purpose in creation was to create [1] and to maintain [2] a universal community [3] in which there is creativity [4] and productivity [5] in an environment of health,[6] peace [7] and harmony .[8] Creation is the absolute origination of all things by the great triune God in which He spoke into existence (before anything existed) the heavens and the earth and all that they contain. The entirety of His creation (visible, invisible, natural and supernatural) is virtually held together by the word of His power. [9] All things were created according to His will, for His glory and for the accomplishment of His eternal purposes. [10] The origin and ultimate purpose of creation can never be discovered by the natural mind, since it is a mystery of God that can only be understood by the mind of faith. [11]

1-(Gen. 1:1); 2-(Col. 1:17); 3-(Eph. 1:10; 3:14-15); 4-(Gen. 2:19); 5-(Gen. 1:28; 2:15); 6-(Ex. 15:26); 7-(Is. 9:6-7; 2 Thess. 3:16); 8-(1 Cor. 1:10); 9-(Col. 1:16-17; Heb. 1:3); 10-(Eph. 1:11; Rev. 4:11); 11-(Heb. 11:3).

B. Of the Angels and Original Sin

God created the entire angelic host as moral spirit beings, originally good in nature, for the purpose of serving and worshiping Him in the freedom of their wills.[1] Rebellion (the original sin against God) first entered God's creation through the angel Lucifer (also named Satan and the devil).[2] Because of pride and selfish ambition, he exalted himself against God and swept away a third of the angels in deception. [3] God did not tempt or cause Lucifer to sin nor should God ever be considered the author of sin. [4] It was in the freedom of Lucifer's own will and in his self-exalted pride that he chose to rebel against God.[5] As a result, Satan and his evil kingdom of fallen angels (demons) were cast out of heaven and confined to the earth. [6] The devil, along with his angels and all whom he can deceive, continue to oppose and war against the Kingdom of God, attempting to steal, kill and destroy God's purposes on earth.[7] Nevertheless, Satan's evil kingdom and all that follow him will ultimately be defeated and undergo final judgment by God. [8]

1-(Gen. 1:31; 2:1; Heb. 1:13-14; Rev. 5:11-14); 2-(John 8:44; 1 John 3:8); 3-(Is. 14:12-15; Ezek. 28:12-17; Rev. 12:3-4); 4-(James 1:13; 1 John 3:5); 5-(2 Pet. 2:4; Jude 6); 6-(Is. 14:12; Ezek. 28:17; Rev. 12:7-9); 7-(John 10:10; Eph. 6:12). 8-(Rev. 11:15; 19:20; 20:10-15).

C. Of the Earth

God created the earth to be a physical (time /space) and metaphysical (subject to spirit interaction) world[1] upon which He unfolds His marvelous plans, carries out His eternal decrees, and reveals the mysteries of His Kingdom.[2] When Satan and his angels were cast to the earth, they brought the spiritual chaos and disorder of their evil kingdom to the physical world. [3] Man, according to his original purpose, was placed on the earth as God's representative through whom He purposes to restore order and control to the planet.[4] The earth and all creation have been subjected to the consequences of sin and, as such, groan under its weight until God's restoration is accomplished through man.[5] Since the earth is the Lord's by virtue of

His purposeful creation, He will most certainly destroy the destroyer of the earth.[6] God will, upon the return of Christ at the end time, purge all sin from the earth and provide a new heaven and a new earth where resurrected man will dwell with Him forever.[7]

1-(Gen. 1:1-31; Col. 1:16); 2-(Num. 14:21; Matt. 13:11; Eph. 1: 9-11;); 3-(Is. 14:17; 45:18; Gen. 1:2; Jer. 4:23); 4-(Gen. 1:28; 2:15; Ps. 8:3-6): 5-(Rom. 8:19-23); 6-(Ps. 24:1; Rev. 11:18); 7-(Rev. 21:1-4).

D. Of Man and Woman and their Purpose

God, by the solemn counsel of His will, created man to be in His image and likeness (i.e. His character, nature, and purpose). [1] Man is therefore a triune being consisting of spirit (God's nature and character that governs his being), soul (mind, will and emotions) and body (the earthen vessel suitable for life on the earth and able to "house" man's spirit and soul).[2] God's original purpose for man was to be an earthly vessel through whom order could be brought to the chaos and rebellion caused by satanic forces. God charged man to represent His rule on the earth by bearing witness to God's Kingdom and resisting Satan's authority through godly obedience, dominion and rule. [3] God made woman from man to be a comparable helper (Heb: an "ally" in time of war) for accomplishing His purposes on the earth.[4] God's intention was for the man (the masculine image of God) and the woman (the feminine image of God) to work together with such unity of purpose that they would reflect the full counsel of God in all that they do. In addition, the relationship between a man and his wife was intended by God to be an earthly demonstration of the love, trust and commitment that He desires His people to have toward Him.[5]

1-(Gen. 1:26); 2-(1 Thess. 5:23); 3-(Gen. 1:26-28; Ps. 8:3-6; Mal. 4:3; Rom. 16:20); 4-(Gen. 2:18-25; Matt. 19:4-6); 5-(Eph. 5:22-32; 1 Pet. 3:7-9).

E. Of the Fall of Man

In their original state, our first parents (Adam and Eve) were upright in character and obedient in nature. Though they had no preference or desire to transgress the will of their Creator, God made them to be free moral agents with the power to choose to obey or to defy His will. [1] Furthermore, Adam was the father of the human race and the representative head of all his descendants, which meant that the power of his choice would affect his total posterity. [2] The entrance of Satan into the Garden of Eden was allowed by God for the purpose of giving man his first opportunity to fulfill his divine commission. God had created Adam for the purpose of being obedient, taking dominion, subduing and ruling over the earth and guarding the Garden of Eden against intrusion.[3] Satan, in keeping with his evil intention to destroy God's purposes, tempted Adam and Eve. Through deception he enticed them to disobey the will of God.[4] The result was that man lost his innocence, fell into sin and was driven from the presence of God.[5] Consequently, not only Adam and Eve, but the entire human race acquired a corrupt nature, inclined always toward evil and incapable of reclaiming their original relationship with God by any works of the flesh. [6] Thus, Adam failed in his original purpose to overcome satanic authority on the earth and instead he became a slave to sin and to the devil. [7]

1-(Gen. 1:26,31; 2:16-17; Eccles. 7:29); 2-(Gen. 3:16-19; Rom. 5:12,14); 3-(Gen. 1:26-28; 2:15; 3:1); 4-(Gen. 3:1-7; John 10:10; 2 Cor. 11:3); 5-(Gen. 3:7-8, 22-24); 6-(Ps. 51:5; Rom. 7:18-21; Eph. 2:1); 7-(John 8:34; 2 Tim. 2:26).

F. Of the Promise and Necessity for the Redemption of Fallen Man

In the sovereign and unchangeable purposes of God,[1] He has chosen to demonstrate the superiority of His power, mercy and grace by redeeming man from the destruction of sin.[2] In the infinite foreknowledge of Almighty God,[3] He knew, even prior to the occasion of sin, that man would fall by satanic temptation. Therefore, in His unsearchable wisdom, God predetermined that He would deposit the treasure of His eternal purposes in the frailty and brokenness of human vessels.[4] Herein is divine wisdom: God ultimately defeats Satan by the witness of his own victim (man) whom God has both redeemed and restored.[5] Thus the decrees and promises of salvation that are given in Scripture are both necessary to the accomplishment of God's eternal purposes and fully secured by the predetermined plan of redemption in Christ Jesus.[6]

1-(Heb. 6:17-18); 2-(Rom. 3:23-25; 1 Tim. 1:16-17); 3-(Rom. 11:33-34); 4-(Rom. 8:29-30; 2 Cor. 4:6-7); 5-(Gen. 3:14-15; Rom. 16:20; Eph. 3:10-11); 6-(Luke 24:25-27; Acts 2:23-24).

IV. THE REDEMPTION OF MAN

A. Of Salvation

Salvation [1] is an inclusive word that gathers into itself all the redemptive acts [2] and processes of God toward fallen man: i.e. Calling, [3] Regeneration, [4] Conversion, [5] Justification, [6] Adoption, [7] Sanctification, [8] Perseverance, [9] and Glorification. [10] In the truest definition of the word (according to the original languages), salvation implies the ideas of deliverance from an enemy, rescue from a hopeless situation and restoration to a place of safety.[11] Thus, the purpose of salvation is to rescue fallen man from all that would ruin his soul, to regain his access to God's presence,[12] and to restore him to God's original purpose.[13] Through salvation, man can again become God's representative on the earth to witness against Satan's evil kingdom [14] with the ultimate end of returning the kingdom of the world to the kingdom of God and His Christ (which was his original mission).[15]

1-(Acts 4:12); 2-(Eph 1:7); 3-(Rom. 8:30); 4-(Titus 3:5-6); 5-(Matt. 18:3); 6-(Rom. 5:18); 7-(Eph. 1:5);8-(2 Thess. 2:13); 9-(Rom. 2:7); 10-(Phil. 3:20-21); 11-(Col. 1:13-14); 12-(Heb. 10:19-22); 13-(Gen. 1:28; 3:15; Rom 16:20); 14-(Matt. 24:14; Eph. 3:10); 15-(1 Cor. 15:24; Rev. 11:15).

B. Of the Covenant Of Redemption

The Covenant of Redemption is that great eternal covenant made between the persons of the Trinity before the foundations of the world decreeing that fallen man would be redeemed from his sinful state. [1] In this great Trinitarian Covenant, the Father is the originator of the decree. The

Son voluntarily takes the place of fallen man becoming the ultimate sacrifice for the sin of all mankind, [2] and the Holy Spirit applies the saving work of the Son to the hearts of believers.[3] Hence, redemption has its conception, implementation, and culmination secured with an irrevocable eternal covenant made by God Himself, who cannot lie.[4]

1-(Eph. 1:4, 11; 3:11; 2 Thess. 2:13); 2-(Ps. 2:7-9; John 6:38-40; 10:17-18; 17:4); 3-(John 14:26; 16:13-15; 1 John 5:7-9); 4-(Heb. 6:13-20; Num. 23:19).

C. Of the Covenant Of Grace

The Covenant of Grace is that merciful agreement initiated by a gracious God to the offending sinner that extends the promise of salvation through faith in Christ to the sinner without any merit on his part.[1] Grace (divine empowerment unto salvation) is freely extended to all men[2], but effectual salvation is received only by those who respond in faith [3] to Christ's work on Calvary's cross [4]. Without the two great Trinitarian Covenants of Redemption and Grace, fallen mankind would be eternally lost in his sins without any hope whatsoever of salvation.

1-(Eph. 2:4-9); 2-(1 Tim. 2:3-4; Titus 2:11); 3-(Heb. 4:1-2; 2 Pet. 1:2-11); 4-(1 Cor. 1:18).

D. Of the Substitutionary Atonement

God is infinite in His holiness and righteousness yet equally infinite in His mercy and love. Man, on the other hand, has become spiritually and morally bankrupt–hopelessly in bondage to sin. Therefore, the only way for man to be saved and still maintain the holiness and justice of God is through the Substitutionary Atonement. [1] Knowing that fallen man is depraved[2] and totally unable [3] to fulfill the righteous requirements of the law by his own efforts, Christ satisfied the justice of the law by substituting Himself for man. Thus our sin, guilt and judgment have been atoned and transferred to Him who received the full weight of God's wrath and punishment in our stead. [4] In order to satisfy Adam's failure in obedience, Christ (the Last Adam) became fully obedient to both the law and to God on man's behalf. [5] In this most extraordinary demonstration of God's love and grace, [6] He not only transferred the spiritual failures of all mankind to Christ, who was undeserving of sin, but He also transferred Christ's own holiness and righteousness to man who was unworthy. [7] Thus, through the Substitutionary Atonement, God became the propitiation for the sins of all the world and by faith in His gracious work, we are saved. [8] Through the Son's wondrous work, all that is necessary for redemption and reconciliation to God has been made available to fallen man. [9] Consequently, man now has the potential of being fully restored to the purposes for which God created him.

1-(Ps. 85:10); 2-(Rom. 7:18; Eph. 4:17-19); 3-(1 Cor. 2:14; Eph. 2:1); 4-(Is. 53:4-6; Rom. 8:3-4; 1 Pet. 3:18); 5-(Rom. 5:19; Heb. 5:8-9); 6-(Rom. 5:7-8); 7-(Rom. 5:8; 2 Cor. 5:21); 8-(Rom. 3:23-25; 1 John 2:2); 9-(Rom. 5:11; Col. 1:13-14).

E. Of the Method of Calling People to Salvation

Salvation is made possible only by the prevenient grace of God that reaches to fallen man inviting him to salvation. [1] The grace of God, which has appeared to all men, [2] calls people to salvation through the preaching of the Word of God concerning repentance[3] and faith in the Lord Jesus Christ.[4] By responding in faith to God's grace, people are saved by the washing of regeneration and by the renewing of the Holy Spirit. Being justified by grace through faith, they become heirs of God according to the hope of eternal life. [5]

1-(Eph. 2:8); 2-(Titus 2:11); 3-(1 Cor. 1:21-23; Luke 24:47); 4-(Rom. 10:8-10); 5-(Rom. 3:28; Titus 3:5-7).

F. Of the Evidence of Salvation

The inward evidence of salvation is the inner witness of faith toward Jesus Christ produced by the indwelling Person of the Holy Spirit. [1] The outward evidence of salvation is manifested as a "new life" in Christ [2] which demonstrates love to one another, [3] righteous and holy living [4] and the fruit of the Spirit. [5] Understanding that no man is without sin, [6] the evidence of salvation is specifically seen through true repentance (i.e. changing kingdoms) as believers are delivered from the domain of darkness and transferred to the kingdom of God's beloved Son. Thus, the believer forsakes their sins, as they become known, seeks God's forgiveness and forgives their fellowman.[7]

1-(Rom. 8;16; 1 John 5:7-10); 2-(II Cor. 5:17; Col. 3:10); 3-(John 13:34-35; I John 4:20-21); 4-(Eph. 4:24); 5-(Gal. 5:22-23); 6-(Rom. 3:23); 7-(Acts 26:18-20; Col. 1:13-14; Eph. 4:25-32; Matt. 6:14-15).

G. Of the Final Result and Purpose of Salvation

The final result and purpose of salvation for the individual produces a life that is freed from the power of the devil [1] and gifted by the Holy Spirit to serve and fulfill his or her divine mission on the earth. [2] Thus, the saved man or woman is being restored to become an effective witness for the Kingdom of God and against the kingdom of

Satan.[3] When believers have finished their assigned course on the earth, their spirit/soul will immediately be transported to heaven and into the presence of God to live for eternity. [4] There the believer receives the final reward for faithfulness and joins that heavenly cloud of witnesses anticipating the consummation of all things. [5]

1-(Heb. 2:14-15); 2-(Rom. 12:6-11; 1 Tim. 4:14-16; 2 Tim 4:5); 3- (Matt. 24:14; Acts 1:8; Col. 1:10-14); 4-(Eccles. 12:7; 2 Cor. 5:8- 10); 5-(2 Tim. 4:6-8; Heb. 12:1; Rev. 6:9-11).

THE REDEMPTION OF MAN

V. JESUS CHRIST

A. Of His Person and Nature

The dual nature of Jesus Christ is a spiritual mystery. It is understandable only by faith and has meaning only in light of His mission and work on the earth. Jesus Christ is the Son of God, eternally begotten of the Father, [1] meaning that He is Deity. [2] He is fully God, being the second person of the Trinity, equal to[3] yet separate from the Father [4] and second only in His role in redemption. He not only pre-existed all creation, but also was the creative agent of the Godhead through whom all things came into being. [5] Jesus Christ was also fully man, born of a woman, [6] being God yet without ceasing to be man. He is the incarnation of God [7] (God in the flesh without ceasing to be God) and is the express image of the Father.[8] In His earthly existence, He was supernaturally conceived by the Holy Spirit[9] and born of the virgin Mary,[10] yet He had all human limitations and the total nature of man [11] as Adam prior to the fall of mankind into sin.[12] Christ is one person with two natures flowing through His personality, unconfused, without conflict, yet each working in one person to fulfill His eternal role of redemption.

1-(Ps. 2:7; Mark 1:1; Rom. 1:3-4); 2-(Is. 9:6; Titus 2:13; 1 John 5:20); 3-(John 10:30); 4-(John 8:42); 5-(John 17:5, 24; John 1:3; Col. 1:15-17); 6-(Gal. 4:4); 7-(John 1:1,2,14); 8-(Col. 1:15; Heb. 1:3); 9-(Matt. 1:18; Luke 1:31, 35); 10-(Is. 7:14; Matt. 1:23); 11-(Phil. 2:7-8); 12-(1 Cor. 15:45-48; 2 Cor. 5:21).

B. Of His Mission and Work as King of God's Kingdom

Jesus Christ is King of the Kingdom of God, installed as

the "King Eternal" by God the Father. [1] As the Son of God, He has been set forth by His Father to be the ruling authority over all creation both in heaven and on earth. [2] His mission as King is to abolishing all evil rule and authority and to return the kingdom of the world, which was lost in Satan's rebellion, to the full dominion of the Father. [3] Satan's evil kingdom (demonic forces, fallen rulers and wicked people of the earth) vainly oppose and war against the rule of Christ. [4] God, however, guarantees ultimate victory for His King by giving Him a Kingdom that cannot be overthrown, [5] having the power to ultimately destroy the works of the devil and overcome all opposing forces. [6] The earthly instrument through which Christ carries out His mission and work is His Church. Having been given all authority in heaven and on earth, Christ builds His Church [7] by redeeming fallen men and women from Satan's domain of darkness and returning them to His Kingdom of light. [8] When His work is accomplished, meaning that the witness of the Church is complete and evil has been overthrown, [9] the King will share the inheritance of His Kingdom with His Church, [10] His eternal "Bride". Together they shall rule and reign in the universe forever.[11]

1-(Ps. 2:6-7; 1 Tim. 1:17); 2-(1 Tim. 6:14-16; Matt. 28:18); 3-(Luke 19:10; Rev. 11:15; 1 Cor. 15:24-25); 4-(Ps. 2:1-9; Rev. 19:19); 5-(Dan. 2:44; Heb. 12:26-28); 6-(1 John 3:8; Rev. 17:14); 7-(Matt. 16:18-19); 8-(Col. 1:13; 1 Pet. 2:9); 9-(Phil. 2:9-11; Rev. 12:11; 19:15-16); 10-(Rom. 8:16-17; Eph. 1:9-11; 5:5); 11-(Rev. 21:1-3, 9-10; 22:1-5).

C. Of His Mission and Work as Redeemer
Jesus Christ is the incarnation of the Son of God who came from heaven into the world to destroy the works of the

devil [1] and restore the mission of humankind that was lost through sin. [2] In His messianic role of redemption, Christ, by necessity, had to be God in order to render a sacrifice of infinite value, freeing others from the curse of the law that resulted from sin [3] and from the power of the devil. [4] He also, by necessity, had to be a representative flesh and blood man who could stand for the entire human race, [5] vicariously bearing the full penalty of sin [6] through suffering in body and soul. [7] In the redemptive work of Christ, it is essential to understand that His torturous death on the cross was not a tragic turn of events by chance, but was the predetermined plan of God whereby sin was atoned and death was defeated. [8] Jesus had to qualify Himself for His mission by maintaining perfect obedience [9] to God's laws and living a totally sinless life [10] while experiencing every temptation known to man. [11] Christ, as the "Last Adam", became successful in His mission to overcome Satan, where the first man, Adam, failed. [12] Thus, by purchasing the redemption of fallen man through His shed blood[13] on the cross of Calvary, Jesus Christ saves all that respond to Him in faith. [14] All who are redeemed by the Lord are set free from the power of the devil [15] and are restored [16] to their original mission—representing God's Kingdom on the earth and bearing witness against Satan's evil kingdom. [17] Furthermore, ultimate humiliation is inflicted upon Satan in that Christ overcomes him, through the hand of his own victim. [18] And as a final declaration of the Redeemer's victory over sin and the devil, Christ, upon His death, descended into the realms of the departed where He proclaimed His triumph to the spirit world. [19]

1-(1 John 3:8); 2-(Luke 19:10); 3-(Ps.. 49:7-9; Gal. 3:13; Rom. 5:12, 15) 4-(Acts 26:18; Col. 1:13-14); 5-(Rom. 8:3-4; Heb. 2:17-

18); 6-(2 Cor. 5:21; Rom. 6:23; 1 Pet. 3:18); 7-(Acts 3:18); 8-(Is. 53:3-6; Matt. 16:21; Acts 2:23-24; Rev. 13:8); 9-(Heb. 5:8-9); 10-(2 Cor. 5:21; Heb. 7:26-28); 11-(Heb. 4:15); 12-(Rom. 5:14-15; 1 Cor. 15:45-47); 13-(Heb. 9:14, 22); 14-(Rom. 3:25-26; 10:8-11; Heb. 4:16); 15-(Heb. 2:14); 16-(Gal. 2:20); 17-(Gen. 1:26-28; Eph. 3:10); 18-(Rom. 16:20; Rev. 12:11); 19-(Eph. 4:9; 1 Pet. 3:19-22; Col. 2:15).

D. Of His Resurrection, Post Resurrection Ministry and Exaltation

After His sacrificial death on the cross, the body of Jesus was buried and remained in the tomb for three days.[1] On the third day, God raised Him from the dead and He showed Himself alive in bodily form to many witnesses.[2] During the forty days following His resurrection and prior to His ascension, Jesus continued to teach and exhort His disciples specifically about the things of the Kingdom of God.[3] The understanding and impact of this final message of Christ was so powerful that the Kingdom became an integral part of the disciples' preaching and teaching throughout the entire apostolic period. [4] The resurrection of Christ from the dead was more than a return to physical life. In it, human purpose was restored, salvation was completed, and the devil and death were rendered powerless. [5] The fact of the resurrection is essential to salvation. Without it, the atoning work of Christ would have died with Him; our faith would be in vain, and man would have no assurance of a personal resurrection in the future. [6] Because of His obedience to His redemptive mission, God has highly exalted Jesus Christ. There is salvation in no name under heaven other than His. [7] As a physical evidence of His exaltation, the resurrected Christ ascended bodily into heaven in full view of His disciples and returned to the

Father who sent Him. [8] The exalted Christ is now seated at the right hand of the Father where He lives forever making intercession [9] for the Church, His Bride, to accomplish her mission of bearing witness of God's kingdom on the earth. [10]

1-(Matt. 12:40; 1 Cor. 15:3-4); 2-(Acts 2:31-32; 10:39-41); 3-(Acts 1:3); 4-(Acts 8:12; 19:8; 20:27; 28:23, 31; Heb. 12:28; James 2:5; 2 Pet. 1:11; Rev. 11:15); 5-(Acts 1:8; Rom. 6:5-6; Heb. 2:14-15); 6- (1 Cor. 15:12-19); 7-(Phil. 2:8-11; Acts 4:12); 8-(Acts 1:9-11; 2:32-33); 9-(Rom. 8:34; Heb. 7:25); 10-(Matt. 24:14; Rom. 16:20; Heb. 10:12-13).

E. Of His Return to the Earth

Scripture clearly indicates that Jesus Christ will physically return to the earth as was declared by Jesus Himself, [1] the angels of God, [2] and the apostles. [3] As to the day or the hour of His return, no man knows. [4] However, the Church (who continues Christ's mission on earth) is God's essential factor in bringing about His return. When Christ had accomplished His redemptive work on earth, He ascended into heaven and "sat down at the right hand of God, waiting from that time onward until His enemies are made a footstool for His feet".[5] Christ's Church is His Body on earth and is, as such, the human agency through whom God defeats Satan. [6] Therefore, before Christ can come again, the Church must fulfill her assignment of doing the works of Christ throughout the earth, [7] making disciples of all the nations [8] and becoming the mature Bride comparable to her Husband. [9] Christ will not return to the earth until His Church effectively demonstrates the Gospel of the Kingdom as a witness to the nations, [10] restores that which was lost, [11] and overcomes the devil. [12] It would be a mistake to presume that His return may be in secret or perhaps only to a select few. [13] The return of Christ will be personal, [14] physical, visible, [15] and gloriously triumphant [16] such that the whole earth will know that it is Christ Himself. [17] As to the purpose of Christ's return, He will come to consummate the final redemption of His people through resurrection and glorification, [18] to utterly destroy all that is evil and to usher in His eternal kingdom of righteousness on the earth as it is in heaven. [19]

1-(John 14:2-3); 2-(Acts 1:9-11); 3-(1 Thess. 2:19; James 5:7-8; 2 Pet. 3:4-13); 4-(Mark 13:32; Acts 1:7); 5-(Heb. 10:12-13); 6-(Gen. 3:15; Luke 10:19; Rom. 16:20); 7-(Luke 4:18; Acts 1:6-8); 8-(Matt. 28:19-20); 9-(Rev. 19:7-8; 21:2); 10-(Matt. 24:14); 11-(Acts 3:21); 12-(Eph. 6:10-17; Rev. 12:11); 13-(Matt. 24:4-6, 23-28); 14-(1 Thess. 4:16); 15-(Acts 1:11); 16-(2 Thess. 1:7; Titus 2:13); 17-(Matt. 24:27-31); 18-(Matt. 24:31; 1 Cor. 15:50-54; 1 Thess 4:16-17; Rom 8:17; 2 Thess. 1:10); 19-(Matt. 6:10; Rev. 20:10-15; 21:3-4; 22:3-5).

VI. THE HOLY SPIRIT

A. Of His Person

The Holy Spirit is the third Person of the Trinity (third only in His role of redemption), equal to God in His essence (deity), yet distinct in His person and work. [1] The Holy Spirit proceeds from both the Father and the Son (thus He is called both the "Spirit of God" and the "Spirit of Christ") [2] and possesses the nature, character, perfection, and attributes of God. He is the "Resident God" on earth sent by Jesus to dwell in the hearts of believers and empower them for service. [3] The Holy Spirit is peaceful and gentle in nature, patiently and lovingly drawing sinners to Christ and to the grace of redemption.[4] Because the work of the Holy Spirit is essential in the salvation process, He is to be honored and received with all attentiveness. Therefore, it is imperative to understand that the Holy Spirit can be easily grieved, [5] quenched [6] or even insulted. [7] The tragedy of consistent resistance or rebellion against His work will result in destruction, death, or even Hell itself. [8]

1-(Gen. 1:2; Matt. 28:19; Eph. 4:30); 2-(John 15:26; Rom. 8:9); 3-(John 14:16-17; 15:26; Acts 1:8); 4-(Gal. 5:22-23; John 12:32; 16:13-15); 5-(Eph. 4:30); 6-(1 Thess. 5:19); 7-(Heb. 10:29); 8-(Is. 63:10; Matt. 12:31-32; Acts 5:3-10; Heb.6:4-6).

B. Of His Work in Creation and Redemption

The Holy Spirit is the "Executive" Agent of the Godhead who is credited with the general acts of creation, [1] giving of life, [2] providential care, [3] giving of inspiration and revelation, [4] and the dispensing of common grace to all men regardless of their spiritual condition. [5] Specifically, however, the Holy Spirit is the active Agent in the work of redemption. He is the One who brings conviction of sin to the hearts of men and women and reveals to them the redemptive work of Christ. [6] He is present at regeneration and is the Originator of new life in the believer. [7] The Holy Spirit is the Executor of the process of sanctification[8] through which we become partakers of His divine nature and are able to persevere to the end, even in the midst of suffering. [9] The indwelling Spirit of God teaches, guides, comforts, and corrects the believer [10] by means of the Word of God, prayer and self-examination. Finally, the wondrous power of the Holy Spirit is not only available during the believer's life but is also instrumental after our physical death. On that great day of resurrection, the same Spirit of God who raised Jesus from the dead will also unite the souls of the redeemed with new glorified bodies and they will live forever in His presence and in His heavenly Kingdom. [11]

1-(Gen. 1:2; Ps. 104:30); 2-(Gen. 2:7; Job 33:4); 3-(Ps. 139:1-12; 104:14, 21, 28); 4-(Eph. 1:17; 2 Pet. 1:20-21); 5-(Gen. 8:22; Matt. 5:45); 6-(John 16:8-15); 7-(John 3:5-8; 2 Cor. 5:17); 8-(1 Thess. 5:19-23; 2 Thess. 2:13); 9-(2 Pet. 1:3-11; Matt. 10:17-22; Rom. 5:3-5); 10-(John 14:16, 17, 23-26); 11-(Rom. 8:11; 1 Cor. 15:35-57; Rev. 21:1-7).

C. Of His Mission and Work in the Church

The Spirit of God has always been the Prime Mover and Enabler for the will of God to be carried out through His people on earth.[1] In the Old Testament, the Holy Spirit came upon, filled and energized God's people to accomplish their divinely appointed purposes. [2] However, it was not until the outpouring of the Holy Spirit on the day of Pentecost that He came to permanently abide with and in those whom Christ had redeemed. [3] At Pentecost, the Church which Jesus had built, was empowered and unified to accomplish her assignment to be a witness for Christ and His Kingdom throughout all the world. [4] Just as He prepared and anointed Jesus for His earthly ministry, [5] the Holy Spirit also prepares the Church to be Christ's Bride [6] by conforming and transforming her into His image. [7] It is the Holy Spirit who dispenses spiritual gifts to the Church[8] and anoints her leaders for effectual ministry. [9] The Holy Spirit is the One who reveals the hidden purposes of God to the Church, guides her into all truth and empowers her to be a witness of His Kingdom. [10] It is the Spirit of Christ who calls and commissions Apostles, Prophets, Evangelists, Pastors and Teachers to do the work of equipping and maturing Christian churches throughout the world until they all attain the unity of the faith. [11] And it is the Holy Spirit who breathes life into the Church, transcends local denominations and gathers her into one exceedingly great army of God to accomplish His purposes on earth. [12] The final work of the Holy Spirit is to stir the "Bride" with a prophetic knowing and an eager expectation of the season of the return of her "Bridegroom". [13] Thus, both the Spirit and the Bride in a holy agreement continue to make imperative invitational cries to all the world to come to Christ and enter His Kingdom before that great and awesome day of the Second Coming of our Lord.[14]

1-(Zech. 4:6; Mark 16:20; Acts 1:8); 2-(Ex. 31:2-5; 1 Sam. 10:6; Ezek. 11:24); 3-(John 14:16-17, 23; Rom. 8:9-11); 4-(Acts 1:8; 2:1-11); 5-(Luke 4:18-19; Acts 10:38); 6-(John 14:16-21; Eph. 5:22-32; Rev. 19:7-8; 21:2, 9); 7-(Rom. 8:29; 12:1-2); 8-(1 Cor. 12:1-11); 9-

(Eph. 4:11-12; 1 John 2:20, 27); 10-(Deut. 29:29; Amos 3:7; 1 Cor. 2:6-13; John 6:12-15; Acts 1:8); 11-(1 Cor. 12:11, 25-28; Eph. 4:11-16); 12-(Ezek. 37:1-11; Rev. 19:7-14); 13-(Luke 2:25-26; Matt. 16:3; 25:6-10; 1 Thess. 5:1-6; Titus 2:13); 14-(Matt. 24:14, 33; Rev. 22:27).

D. Of the Gifts of the Holy Spirit

When the Lord Jesus Christ completed His earthly work of redemption and established His Church, He returned to the Father in heaven and sent the Holy Spirit to empower the Church to accomplish her assignment and purpose. [1] The Holy Spirit is the Giver of spiritual gifts, distributing them to individuals in the Church just as He desires, for the edification of all. [2] The Holy Spirit gifts some to be leaders in the Church for the purpose of giving guidance, counsel, and equipping Christians to be unified in the work of the ministry. These Leadership Gifts are set in the Church as Apostles, Prophets, Evangelists, Pastors and Teachers.[3] To others, the Holy Spirit grants extraordinary abilities to function in the supernatural realm with unmistakable signs of God's favor toward His people. The Supernatural Manifestations of the Holy Spirit are the word of wisdom, the word of knowledge, faith, healing, miracles, prophecy, discernment of spirits, kinds of tongues, and the interpretation of tongues.[4] Then, to others, the Holy Spirit distributes measures of faith according to the grace given, in order that natural abilities and inclinations are faithfully dedicated to the benefit of God's people and the work of the Church. These gifts include boldly speaking God's Word, serving and helping others, teaching, exhorting, giving, leading, administrating, and showing mercy. [5] It is imperative to understand that all of the gifts of the Holy Spirit are for the common good of the whole Church and are not to be claimed for personal gain nor should they produce jealousy [6] within the church. When the gifts of the Holy Spirit are in proper use in the Church, then each person does his or her part in building up the Church with love.[7]

1-(John 14:12-17; Acts 1:8; 2:4); 2-(1 Cor. 12:4-7, 11, 18); 3-(Eph. 4:7-16; 1 Cor. 12:28); 4-(1 Cor. 12:4-11; 28); 5-(Rom 12:1-8; 1 Cor. 12:28); 6-(1 Cor. 12:7, 12-18; 14:26, 40); 7-(Eph. 4:15-16; Gal. 5:22-23).

VII. ANGELS

A. Of the Origin and Nature of Angels

Angels are spirit beings [1] (not flesh and blood) created prior to man by God as His heavenly host. [2] Angels are immortal, [3] very powerful [4] yet finite [5] creatures, who were originally created morally good [6] but with the capability of freely choosing good or evil.[7] The nature and purpose of angels are different from humans in that there is no need for marriage or reproduction. [8] Angels do, however, have the ability to converse with humans [9] and are sent by God to assist them in time of need. [10] In keeping with God's order and structure in creation, He created His heavenly host in a hierarchical ordering with specific assignments and levels of authority according to His purposes. [11]

1-(Heb. 1:14); 2-(Gen. 2:1; Job 38:4-7; Col. 1:16); 3-(Luke 20:36); 4-(2 Kings 19:35; 2 Thess. 1:7); 5-(Matt. 24:36); 6-(Gen. 1:31; 1 Tim. 4:4); 7-(Jude 6; 2 Pet. 2:4); 8-(Mark 12:25); 9-(Judges 6:12; Luke 1:19); 10-(Ps. 91:11; Matt. 4:11); 11-(Luke 1:19; Col. 1:16; 1 Thess. 4:16; Jude 9).

B. Of the Mission and Purpose of Angels

God created the angelic host for the pleasure of His will, [1] to perform His word and to carry out divine purposes. [2] The primary activity of angelic beings is to serve and worship God forever in the freedom of their wills. [3] Some angels, however, are agents of God's providential work toward human kind sent to communicate God's will, [4] minister strength and protection, [5] and execute divine judgment upon evil. [6] Even though angels have great supernatural power and authority, God warns us that they are never to be worshiped nor sought after for divine favor. [7] However, the Church as Christ's Body and co-worker on earth, may appeal to the Father for angelic assistance to war against evil in her work of the Kingdom. [8] Nevertheless, angels (as wondrous as they may be) are merely instruments of God's great power sent for His purpose and His glory. Because of the great authority that God has given angels, those who have violated His trust, disobeyed His will, and have sought authority and glory for themselves, are recipients of God's ultimate wrath and eternal judgment. [9]

1-(Rev. 4:11); 2-(Ps. 103:20; Heb. 1:14); 3-(Ps. 148:2, 5; Luke 2:13-15; Rev. 4:8-11; 5:11-14); 4-(Luke 1:19; Acts 7:53; Rev. 22:6); 5-(Matt. 4:11; Acts 27:22-23; Heb. 1:13-14; Ps. 91:11-12); 6-(2 Kings 19:35; Acts 12:23); 7-(Heb. 1:4-5; Col. 2:18; Rev. 19:4, 10); 8-(Is. 45:11; 2 Kings 6:15-18; Matt. 26:53); 9-(Is. 14:12-15; 2 Pet. 2:4; Jude 6; Rev. 12:4, 7-9; 20:10).

VIII. THE CHURCH
OF THE LORD JESUS CHRIST

A. Of the Purpose, Origin and Nature of the Church
1. God's Purpose for His Church:

The Church, simply stated, is God's human agency redeemed and commissioned to represent His cause and to fulfill His will on the earth. The Church is the community of believers in the Lord Jesus Christ (both locally and globally) who respond with obedience to His call to repentance and who willingly enter into both personal and corporate covenants with Him to accomplish His purposes on the earth.[1] The Church (literally the "called out ones") is comprised of those whom God has called out of the domain of spiritual darkness and has transferred into the righteous Kingdom of His Son.[2] Therefore, God purposes that His Church is to be the *Embassy* of His Kingdom on earth. The Church represents God's righteous government and entreats lost souls to enter the Kingdom of Heaven by being reconciled to God through Christ.[3] God purposes that His Church is to be *Militant* as His spiritual army warring against the devil's spiritual forces of evil, loosening the bonds of wickedness that oppress people and demonstrating the superior wisdom and power of God at work in human vessels.[4] God purposes that His Church is to be *Restorational* as she demonstrates compassion toward confused and hurting people who are lost in sin and offers forgiveness, healing, restoration, solutions and direction for their lives.[5] God purposes that the Church is to be His *Influence* to the world ("Salt and Light"),

Making Disciples of all the Nations and exhorting them to exchange their allegiance from the kingdom of the world (world systems) to the righteous Kingdom of Christ.[6]

1-(Ex. 19:4-6; Is. 62:12); 2-(1 Pet. 2:9-10; Col. 1:13-14); 3-(2 Cor. 5:20; Matt. 23:13); 4-(Matt. 16:16-19; Is. 58:6; 2 Cor. 10:3-6; Eph. 3:9-10; 6:11-17); 5-(Matt. 9:35-38; 13:33; Gal. 6:1-2; Col. 3:12-17); 6-(Matt. 5:13-16; 28:19-20; Ps. 2:1-12; 1 John 2:15-17; Rev. 11:15).

2. The Origin of the Church:

God has always had a Church or "Covenant People" to accomplish His purposes on earth. The Church has appeared in different forms and levels of maturity throughout the ages, but its origin always begins with Covenant. The first expression of God's Church was evident with the creation of mankind and His *Covenant with Adam.* Adam and his children were commissioned to subdue and rule the earth and obey the warnings of God. [1] Through the *Noachic Covenant*, this patriarch and his family typified the Church as they were spared from Divine judgment through the mercy of God and the obedience of Noah. [2] However, the Church in the Old Testament was seen in its greatest clarity with the *Abrahamic Covenant* wherein Abraham was "called out" of an idolatrous nation to a land where he would receive an inheritance. Through his belief and obedience, God blessed Abraham, imputed to him righteousness and promised that his "Seed" would possess the gate of their enemies.[3] God continued to give definition to His Church through His *Covenants with Moses and David.* [4] However, the fullness of the Church was not realized until the advent of God's own Son, Jesus Christ. In Christ, the blessing of Abraham came to all men such that by faith in Him and His redemptive work we inherit the promise of Abraham and become sons of God.[5] Thus, Jesus Christ became the Head of the Church, [6] established her upon the *New Covenant of Redemption*, [7] empowered her with the Holy Spirit to be His witnesses [8] and commissioned her to war against evil and continue His work on earth. [9]

1-(Gen. 1:26-28; 2:16-17; Ps. 8:4-6; Hosea 6:7; Heb. 11:4)); 2-(Gen. 6:17-22; Heb. 11:7); 3-(Gen. 12:1-3; 22:17-18; Gal. 3:6-7; Heb. 11:8-19); 4-(Acts 7:37-38; 15:14-17; 2 Sam. 7:11-16); 5-(Gal. 3:6-29; 4:4-5); 6-(Col. 1:18; Eph. 5:23); 7-(1 Cor. 11:25; Heb. 9:15; 12:24); 8-(Acts 1:6-8); 9-(Matt. 16:18-19; Eph. 6:11-17; John 14:12).

3. The Nature of the Church and Her Members:

The Church is both *visible* (the natural realm organized with human authority) [1] and *invisible* (the realm of faith with Christ as its head). [2] It is both *local* (geographic locations where believers gather)[3] and *universal* (the sum total of all believers past, present and future). [4] Finally, the Church is *transcendent* in nature meaning that it includes the saints who are in heaven [5] as well as those who are on earth. Those who are on the membership roles of a local church, however, do not necessarily determine true membership in God's Church. God's true Church is comprised of those individuals who are genuinely born again of His Spirit and who have been added to the Church by the Lord Himself. [6] Nevertheless, all true members of God's invisible and universal Church will most certainly and willingly become active members of His visible and local Church. [7]

1-(Eph. 4:11-16); 2-(Heb. 11:6; Col. 1:18); 3-(Acts 15:41); 4-(Heb.
11:32-40; Acts 2:39); 5-(Heb. 12:22-23); 6-(John 1:12-13; 3:3-
6; Acts 2:41-47); 7-(Ex. 31:16-17; Heb. 10:19-25).

B. Of the Church as "Spiritual Israel"

1. Israel as the "Chosen People of God":

In the beginning, God created the first human beings as
"His people" to enjoy a personal relationship with Him
and to fulfill their corporate assignment. [1] However, as
a result of Adam's sin of disobedience, the entire human race was estranged from God and driven from His
presence.[2] Yet, because of God's merciful grace and for
the sake of His great name and eternal purposes for
mankind, the Lord did not totally abandon His people
but provided the way for that relationship to be restored
and for the man's mission to be recovered. [3] Thus, God
set forth these conditions: all who respond in *faith* with
heartfelt *obedience* to His voice and who keep His *Covenant* could again become *"the people of God"*.[4]
Abraham was such a person who, in faith, responded to
God with obedience and covenant. Consequently, his
descendants (Israel) came to be known as "a great and
mighty nation of God".[5] However, it is essential to understand that Israel did not become the "chosen people
of God" because of some special favor or innate goodness as a race of people. It was simply because God
loves all men, regardless of their spiritual condition, and
He faithfully promised to restore those who respond to
His covenant and who love Him with all their heart and
soul. [6] Whoever exercises faith in God with obedience
and covenant will be restored and will become the
"People of God". [7]

1-(Gen. 1:26; Ps. 8:4-6); 2-(Gen. 3:8, 23-24); 3-(1 Sam. 12:22; Heb. 13:5); 4-(Ex. 19:5-6; Hosea 1:10); 5-(Heb. 11:8-10; Gen. 18:18-19); 6-(Deut. 7:7-9; 13:3-4; Jer. 7:23; 11:4); 7-(John 1:11-13; 3:16).

2. Israel and the New Covenant:

According to Israel's covenant, a right relationship with God was based upon the yearly shedding of the "sinless blood" of animals and the keeping of the law of God. [1] Even though God knew that fallen man could never maintain his own righteousness by the works of the flesh, He still gave this covenant as a type and a shadow (even a schoolmaster) of a better covenant that would follow.[2] In the fullness of time, God made the "Old Covenant" (the works of the flesh) obsolete and replaced it with the "New Covenant" of justification by faith in God's redemptive work on the behalf of man. [3] God replaced the Old Covenant of circumcision of the flesh with the New Covenant of a spiritual circumcision of the heart.[4] God replaced the Old Covenant of atonement through the blood sacrifices of bulls and goats with the New Covenant of atonement through the shed blood of Christ, the sinless Lamb of God. [5] God replaced the Old Covenant of human obedience to the letter of the Law (which Israel could never do) with a better Covenant of faith in Christ who was, in fact, completely obedient to the Law on our behalf. [6] But, even though Israel was disobedient and did not keep the Old Covenant, [7] God kept His gracious promise and offered to Israel the first opportunity to partake in His New Covenant. [8] However, because of the hardness of their hearts, Israel missed the hour of her visitation from God and refused to accept the Christ of the New Covenant. [9] Consequently, God took His

Kingdom away from them and gave it to those who would produce the fruit of it. [10] Therefore, if national Israel is still holding on to the Old Covenant, then they have no covenant with God and are no longer the "people of God." [11] The natural Jew, as any other human being, has no effectual covenant with God outside of the New Covenant in Christ and must, accordingly, be "grafted in" again by receiving Jesus Christ as both Lord and Savior in order to become the "people of God".[12]

1-(Ex. 19:5-8; Lev. 16:23-34); 2-(Heb. 8:1-6; Gal. 3:25-25); 3-(Rom. 3:21-28; Heb. 8:7-13); 4-(Gen. 17:9-11; Rom. 2:28-29); 5-(Heb. 9:11-15; 10:1-4); 6-(Rom. 5:19-21; 2 Cor. 3:6; Gal. 2:16); 7-(Ps. 81:11-13; Jer. 3:8); 8-(Is. 59:20; Matt. 15:21-24); 9-(Matt. 23:37-39; Luke 19:41-44; Heb. 3:8-12); 10-(Matt. 21:42-43; John 1:11); 11-(Heb. 8:8-10; 1 Pet. 2:4-10); 12-(Jer. 31:31; Rom. 11:7-24; Acts 2:36-41).

3. The New "Israel of God":

God, who is the God of all people, does not show partiality [1] but reaches out to all men regardless of race or nationality with a universal invitation: "whosoever will call upon the name of the Lord will be saved". [2] The "Israel of God" is as it always has been—all people who respond in faith, demonstrate heartfelt obedience to His Word and keep His Covenant. Since the "Old Israel" disqualified herself, then the "New Israel" of God is made up of those who will enter by faith into the New Covenant of Christ's blood and accept His redemptive work on the cross. [3] The Covenant that God established with Abraham and his descendants[4] was fully realized in Christ [5] and all who are baptized into Christ belong to Him and are heirs of God's promises to Abraham. [6]

The Christian Church, through their faith in Christ, is therefore the recipient of all the promises of God and has become the "Spiritual Israel" and the "people of God" through whom He works on planet earth. [7]

1-(Deut. 10:17; Rom. 2:9-13; 3:29-30); 2-(Matt. 11:28-30; Rom. 9:24-26; 10:12-13); 3-(Gal. 6:13-16; Eph. 1:7); 4-(Gen. 17:9,17; 22:18); 5-(Gal. 3:16); 6-(Gal. 3:26-29); 7-(Rom. 9:6-8; 1 Pet. 2:9-10).

C. Of the Church as the "Maturing Bride" and "Wife" of Christ

The Bible presents the relationship between Christ and His Church as a spiritual union similar to the covenant of marriage between a husband and his wife. According to the Biblical imagery, Christ is the Head of His Church, vicariously loving and caring for her and preparing her to be a comparable helper (or ally) for Himself. [1] The Bible, however, never attempts to portray the Church as a sinless or innately righteous people but rather as those who are being cleansed, sanctified and justified by Christ, their Savior. [2] Jesus, upon His ascension into heaven, sent the Holy Spirit as His Enabling Agent to dwell in and work with His redeemed people equipping them for their mission as His Church on earth. [3] The Holy Spirit matures and prepares the Church to be the Bride of Christ by working through the "Five-fold/Ascension Gift" ministries to bring her to the unity of the faith (regardless of race, gender, or denomination) and into the fullness of the image of Christ.[4] In so doing, the world will see a credible witness of a unified Church doing the work of Christ on earth and bearing witness of His Kingdom. [5] The Bride matures and makes herself ready for her Husband by corporately becoming the outstretched hand of Christ—giving hope to a lost and dying world, bringing order, providing solutions to human problems, and proclaiming release to a world enslaved by the power of the devil. [6] When the Church has accomplished her mission of warring against evil, overcoming Satan and influencing the kingdoms of the world for God, then Christ, her Husband, will return again to the earth .[7] Finally, the Church, the Wife of Christ, will come into the fullness of her glory, and she will inherit the Kingdom of God to rule with Him forever in eternity. [8]

1-(Is. 54:4-6; Eph. 5:22-27: Col. 1:18); 2-(1 Cor. 6:9-11); 3-(John 14:16-21, 26); 4-(Rom. 8:29-30; Gal. 3:27-28; Eph. 4:11-16; Rev. 21:2); 5-(John 14:12-14; 17:21); 6-(Rev. 19:7-8; Luke 4:18-19); 7-(Matt. 16:18-19; Eph. 6:10-18; Rev. 11:15; 12:11; Acts 3:20-21); 8-(Matt. 5:3-4; 25:34; 2 Tim. 2:12; Rev. 5:10; Rev. 21:9-27; 22:3-5).

D. Of the Authority of God's Church

1. The Church is Christ's Delegated Authority to Act on His Behalf on Earth:

God the Father has made Jesus Christ to be the head of His Church and has given to Him all authority in heaven and on earth and with the freedom to delegate that authority as He wills.[1] In Scripture, Jesus clearly indicates the level of authority that He gives and expects to see operative in His Church. Just as His Father sent Jesus into the world, so Jesus sends His Church into the world.[2] Just as Jesus is the light of the world, so He declares His Church to be the light of the world.[3] Just as Jesus did works in His Father's name, so He commissions His Church to do even greater works in His name.[4] Just as Jesus came into the world to destroy the works of the devil and restore what was lost, [5] so He gave His Church authority over evil forces and the power to restore those whom the devil has corrupted. [6] Thus, just as Jesus was the authority of His Father in the world, so the Church is the authority of Christ in the world.

1-(Matt. 11:27; 28:18; Col. 1:16-18); 2-(John 17:18; Mark 16:15); 3-(John 8:12; Matt. 5:14-16); 4-(John 10:25; 14:12-14); 5-(1 John 3:8; Luke 19:10); 6-(Matt. 10:1; 2 Cor. 10:3-6; Acts 26:18; Gal. 6:1).

2. The Church has Authority to Bind and Loose According to the Pattern of Heaven:

When Jesus established His Church, He depicted it as being in a violent power struggle against the forces of "Hades" (the abode of sin and wickedness). Consequently, Christ built His Church not only upon the central revelation that He is the Christ but also for the purpose of withstanding spiritual powers of evil. [1] Accordingly, Jesus gave His Church the "Keys" (the authority and power) of His Kingdom for the purpose of demonstrating His authority on earth even as it exists in heaven.[2] The Church, therefore, exercises that authority of Christ's Kingdom by binding and loosing on earth that which has been bound and loosed in heaven. [3] (Literally, according to the Greek grammar: "whatever you shall bind on earth, shall have already been bound in heaven".) The Church uses this authority to stop the workings of evil and to release people from the bondage of wickedness. Knowing the powerful role and the mission of Angels in warring against evil,[4] the Church can appeal to the Father for angelic assistance in spiritual warfare. [5] Furthermore, the Church has been given this great decisive power not only for dealing with demonic forces [6] but also for dealing appropriately with the sins of church members. [7]

1-(Matt. 16:16-18); 2-(Matt. 6:10); 3-(Matt. 16:19); 4-(Dan. 10:12-13; Rev. 12:7-9); 5-(2 Kings 6:15-18; Ps. 91:11-12; Matt. 26:53); 6-(Eph. 6:10-18; James 4:7); 7-(Matt. 18:15-19; John 20:23).

3. The Church has Authority over Evil Spirits and Diseases:

Christ gave His followers the authority to take dominion over evil spirits (including the devil himself) and to heal every kind of disease. [1] According to the very words of Jesus, the casting out of demonic forces is undeniable evidence that the Kingdom of God has come to the earth. [2] It becomes essential, therefore, for the Church to exercise God's authority over evil spirits as a representative of God's righteous rule on earth and as a demonstration that the Church can overcome the works of the devil. In addition, the authority of the Church to heal diseases becomes another sign to the world that the Church represents the authority and power of the Kingdom of God. [3] Not only is healing an expression of God's mercy toward humanity, but it also releases believers from the bondage of <u>sickness </u>in order to serve God in the strength of physical wholeness.[4]

1-(Matt. 10:1; Luke 9:1; Rev. 12:9-11); 2-(Luke 11:20); 3-(Mark 16:15-18); 4-(Matt. 8:14-15; 20:34).

4. The Church has Authority to Declare the Forgiveness of Sins:

God is the ultimate and final authority who forgives sins.

However, Christ has committed to His Church the awesome responsibility of ministering God's reconciliation to sinners and of declaring the forgiveness of sins through His redemptive work.[1] When the risen Christ appeared to the leadership of His newly formed Church, He breathed His Spirit upon them, gave them the authority to declare the terms of salvation, and sent them into the world. Accordingly, the Church not only has the authority to release repentant sinners from their sins (based upon their confession of Christ) but also to declare that without Christ people will remain unforgiven in their sins. [2]

1-(2 Cor. 5:18-20; 1 John 2:12); 2-(John 20:21-23; Rom. 10:8-11; 1 Tim. 1:19-20).

5. The Church has Authority to Discipline its own Members:

As has been previously mentioned, Jesus gave His Church the authority to restrain not only evil spirits but also sinful activities of individuals in the church. [1] It is the Scriptural requirement of Church leadership to be aware of those who blatantly and unrepentantly violate the moral and spiritual standards of Christianity and to bring the appropriate correction and warning to the congregation of their activities. [2] However, Scripture also teaches that the purpose for discipline within the Church is for correction and restoration rather than for punishment only. [3] As an example of this, the Apostle Paul dealt severely with an individual in the Corinthian Church who was living in obvious sin, but afterwards he gave instructions for that person to be restored back to the fellowship of the Church.[4] Furthermore, believers are admonished by Scripture not to take grievances with another Christian to the courts of the world, but rather that the individuals involved should trust the authority of God's Church to properly judge such matters and bring godly restitution. [5]

1-(Matt. 18:15-19); 2-(Rom. 16:17-18; 1 Tim. 5:19-21; Titus 3:9-11); 3-(Gal. 6:1-3; Heb. 12:6-11); 4-(1 Cor. 5:1-5; 2 Cor. 2:6-11); 5-(1 Cor. 6:1-5).

E. Of the Leadership and Government of the Church

The purpose of Church leadership is to hear from God, serve the people, equip them for the work of the ministry, and set a governmental structure in the Church that facilitates the ministry of Christ on earth. [1] The ultimate goal of all leadership is to bring maturity and unity to the Body of Christ, building them up in love and laboring until they become conformed to the image of Christ. [2] When the Church is set in order and functions as God intended, then the character of Christ and the Kingdom of God (His order and rule) will be demonstrated on earth through His people.[3]

1-(Ex. 18:15-23; Matt. 20:25-28; Eph. 4:11-16; 2 Tim. 4:2; Titus 1:5); 2-(1 Tim. 1:5; Eph. 4:11-16; Gal. 4:19); 3-(Matt. 6:9-10).

1. The Leadership of the "Five-fold/Ascension Gift" Ministries:

Christ, the head and cornerstone of His Church, [1] has set Apostles, Prophets, Evangelists, Pastors and Teachers as His delegated authority for the purpose of governing His Church and leading them to maturity. [2] Those who are called by God to the "Five-fold/Ascension Gift"

Ministries are accountable to God for the Apostolic Tradition [3] of guarding the Faith, [4] promoting the unity of the Body of Christ[5] and preserving the discipline of the Church.[6] These leaders are personally responsible to the Lord, by virtue of their calling and anointing as His undershepherds, to watch over the souls of God's people and to warn them of spiritual dangers which may ensnare their lives.[7] Consequently, God requires His people to give honor and to be responsive to the deposit of spiritual authority that He has placed in those over them in the Lord. [8] Those who are called and set forth to these ministries are Ruling Elders in God's Church and are to be supported from the tithes of the people in order that their time and energies may be fully devoted to the work of the Lord. [9]

1-(Rom. 12:4-5; 1 Cor. 12:12-18; Col. 1:16-18; Eph. 2:19-20); 2-(Eph. 4:11-16); 3-(1 Cor. 11:2; 2 Thess. 2:15; 3:6); 4-(2 Tim. 1:13-14; Eph. 4:11-13; Jude 3); 5-(Eph. 4:3-6; John 17:21); 6-(Matt. 18:15-18; Rom. 16:17; 1 Tim. 5:19-21; Titus 3:9-11); 7-(1 Peter 5:1-4; Ezek. 3:17-21); 8-(Heb. 13:17); 9-(1 Cor. 9:6-11; 1 Tim. 5:17; Deut. 18:1-3; Neh. 10:38-39).

2. The Leadership of the Office of the Bishop:

The work of a Bishop, or Presiding Overseer (episkope), is the Scriptural designation of the office of ministry that oversees the work of the Lord in churches in geographic regions. [1] In the historical Church, this office grew to include the leadership and oversight given to other churches and ministries in the Body of Christ at large. Those who are installed to this office are by necessity also called to the Five-fold/Ascension Gift ministries with proven and seasoned works that warrant this level of leadership to the General Church. This office carries both administrative and spiritual authority since the Bishop sets governing standards for those under his care and functions as a "Pastor" to other pastors and ministers. The work of a Bishop has a special emphasis on the unity of the Body of Christ and setting the Church in Biblical order according to the will of Christ. The local church where the Bishop resides is called a "Cathedral" signifying that the seat (or authority) of the Bishop is in residence.

1-(Acts 20:28; 1 Tim. 3:1-7; Titus 1:5-9).

3. The Leadership of the Elder:

The concept of the "Elder" first appears in Scripture in relation to those who are "older" in age and experience and who are honored as having proven authority in their families (heads of households) or in the leadership of ruling over others in civil or religious matters. [1] In the early Church, the Elder, or Presbyter (presbuterous), had this same connotation, but specifically it had reference to those who presided over and gave leadership to Christian churches. [2] In the early days prior to the vast expansion of the Church and the need for a more organizational structure, Elders (presbuterous) were also considered as Overseers or Bishops (episkopos) of churches to guard and shepherd God's Church. [3] Because of the place of honor and responsibility of the Elder, [4] the Apostle Paul set high standards of upright moral character and conduct as conditions for those who are charged by God to diligently care for His Church.[5] Though the Apostles considered themselves to be Elders within the Christian Church, [6] it is obvious that

God grants a distinct authority and revelation to those with Apostolic callings enabling them to establish churches, appoint Elders and Bishops, and bring correction to the Body of Christ. [7] Thus we conclude that the Elder in God's Church represents a deposit of God's authority in human vessels (both men and women) to lead, guide and rule in the House of God after the pattern of Christ, the Good Shepherd. [8] Also, we conclude that "Eldership" is deposited in Apostles, Prophets, Evangelists, Pastors, Teachers, and in the administrative and spiritual office of the Bishop. Finally, we conclude that Eldership is not limited to "full-time", paid clergy but is deposited in those whom God has anointed and has placed His authority for the purpose of leading His Church.

1-(Gen. 50:7; Ex. 3:16; Num. 11:16); 2-(Acts 14:23; 15:4-6, 22-23; 20:17; Titus 1:5); 3-(Titus 1:5-9; Acts 20:17, 28); 4-(1 Tim. 5:17-19; 1 Pet. 5:5); 5-(1 Tim. 3:1-7; Titus 5:1-9; 1 Pet. 5:1-4); 6-(Acts 15:23; 1 Pet. 5:1; Philem. 9); 7-(2 Cor. 2:1-7; Tit. 1:5; 2 Tim. 4:1-4; 2 Cor. 13:10); 8-(John 10:11-15).

4. The Leadership of the Deacon:

The leadership of God's Church could not be fully effective without the support ministry of the Deacon. Deacons are men and women, chosen by reason of their godly character and reputation,[1] who are gifted to serve (diakoneo) [2] in the Church. Those who are called to the "Diaconate" give leadership to the Church by helping to administrate and care for God's people. Most specifically, however, Deacons must have sufficient spiritual maturity to deal with complaints, offenses and discord among the members of the Church. [3] When Deacons are functioning properly in their gifts, they release the Five-fold/Ascension Gift ministers to devote themselves to prayer, to the ministry of the Word and to function fully in their callings. [4]

1-(Acts 6:3; I Tim. 3:8-13); 2-(Rom. 12:6-7); 3-(Acts 6:1-3; 1 Cor. 12:28); 4-(Ex. 18:13-23; Acts 6:3-4).

F. Of the Levitical Ministry (the Support Ministry) in the Church

1. The Levitical Ministry:

According to the Biblical pattern, God chose members of the Levitical order by reason of their zeal and uncompromised stand for His cause. [1] Moreover, the Levites had a special consecrated standing with God as His dedicated possessions [2] commissioned by the Lord as a gift to the priesthood to assist them in their ministry.[3] In keeping with this commission, it is imperative to emphasize that Support Ministries are to enter into the same vision and spirit of those they serve [4] and are called to "support the hands of Moses" as did Aaron and Hur. [5] Furthermore, God holds members of the Levitical order personally accountable for their loyalty and service to leadership, as He did with Korah in the wilderness. [6] In return for their services and support ministry to the priests, the Levites were given care and pay from the tithes of the people. [7] As a continuation of this Old Testament pattern, God also gives special ministry gifts to men and women in the New Testament Church to assist leadership with their duties and minister to the people. [8]

1-(Ex. 32:25-29); 2-(Num. 3:11-13); 3-(Num. 3:5-9; 18:6); 4-(Num. 11:16-17; Matt. 12:25); 5-(Ex. 17:11-13); 6-(Num. 16:1-35); 7-(Num. 18:21-24; Deut. 12:19); 8-(Rom. 12:3-8; 1 Cor. 12:28; Acts 6:1-6).

2. Areas of Service of the Levitical Ministry (Support Ministry) of the Church:

The Church believes that the services of the Levitical Ministry as set forth in the Old Testament and the gifts given to men and women in the New Testament are both valid and necessary in the Church today. These services, whether volunteered or paid, are legitimate ministries of a Church Staff and should be recognized as having a Biblical basis vital to the work of God's Church. The work of these Support Ministries to the Church include the following:

a. Teachers: *(2 Chr. 35:3; Neh. 8:9; Rom.12:3-8; 1 Cor.12:28)*

b. Ministers of praise and worship: *(1 Chr.16:4; 2 Chr. 8:14)*

c. Musicians and singers for worship: *(1 Chr. 9:33-34; 15:16; 2 Chr. 5:12, 7:6)*

d. Personal assistants to the Priests: *(Num. 3:9; 1 Chr. 23:28-32)*

e. Ministry and care for the people: *(Ex. 18:21-22; Rom.12:3-8; 1 Cor. 12:28; Acts 6:106)*

f. Administrators: *(1 Cor. 12:28; Rom. 12:3-8)*

g. Treasurers: *(1 Chr. 26:26-28)*

h. Secretaries (scribes): *(1 Chr. 2:55; 2 Chr.34:13)*

i. Caretakers of the sanctuary: *(Num. 1:49-53; 18:2-4; 1 Chr. 6:48; 23:27-2)*

j. Ushers (gatekeepers): *(1 Chr. 9:17-27; 26:12-19)*

k.Security personnel (Protecting the tabernacle): *(Num. 1:53)*

l. Overseers of constructing and repairing church facilities: *(1 Chr.23: 2-4; Ezra 3:8-9).*

G. Of Women in Ministry and Leadership:

Since the tragedy of Eve's sin in the Garden of Eden, men have had the tendency to view women as "weaker" vessels, "easily deceived" and "incapable" of exercising godly authority. Almost every culture on earth has diminished the rights of women and relegated her to roles of motherhood and menial labor. Unfortunately, even the Christian Church has fallen into this error. Many have isolated Scriptures such as Gen. 3:16-17 and 1 Timothy 2:9-15 and attempted to suppress any possible potential that women may have—excluding them from significant leadership roles in ministry. Discrimination of one gender against another was never God's intention and does not reflect the truth of Scripture. A Biblically balanced view of women in ministry and leadership must include the following basic truths:

1. God's original purpose for men and women (the "pre-fall" model):

When God created the human race, both Adam and Eve possessed the purity of God's image and likeness. And, contrary to the opinions of some, both the man and the woman were commissioned by God to rule and take dominion over the earth. Thus, Adam and Eve were *God's "warrior team"*—commissioned as *co-rulers* to represent God's government (His Kingdom) on the earth. [1] In the wisdom of His plan, God created the man to reflect His masculine image and the woman to reflect His feminine image. In this divine relationship, both were equal in value and worth, but yet each was given a distinct role and assignment to enhance their God-given mission. To the man, God assigned the responsibility of cultivating the garden and guarding it from the hostile world beyond Eden. And it was Adam who received God's strict warning concerning the consequences of disobedience. [2] God made the woman Adam's "ally" (Hebrew for "help-meet"), sharing equally in the war against evil. Eve was his life-long companion—able to bear children and fill the earth with a righteous witness.[3] God created them both for each other—inseparably committed to one another and to their divine mission (bone of bone and flesh of flesh). In their "pre-fall" relationship, there was no competition, power struggle or abuse of authority. Adam was willing to forsake all earthly relationships to care for and protect Eve. And Eve certainly must have experienced personal security and an intimate sense of belonging toward Adam (for it was from Adam that she was made). [4] Both the woman and the man had equal access to God. With their unique gifts and assignments, they ruled with *interdependence*. They were God's crowning creation—designed as an earthly demonstration of mutual love, trust and commitment, which God desires His people to have toward Him. [5]

1-(Gen. 1:26-28); 2-(Gen. 2:15-17); 3-(Gen. 2:18-22); 4-(Gen. 2:23-25); 5-(Eph. 5:21-32).

2. The result of sin and their fall from God's purpose (the "fallen" model):

As a strong point of Biblical clarity, it must be understood that both Adam and Eve sinned—not just the woman! Thus, Satan's plan to disable God's "warrior team" succeeded. Instead of standing together with God to take dominion over Satan, they hid from their Creator and opposed each another—each blaming another.[1] Furthermore, as a part of the curse of sin, men began to rule over women rather than rule with them! (*Note: God did not command men to rule over women—He was simply stating the tragic result of sin.*) [2] Men abrogated their divine roles as protectors and co-rulers and instead became oppressive authority figures exploiting and abusing women. [3] The once life-long monogamous marriage relationship became disfigured with polygamy and divorce.[4] With the breakdown of the divine roles, men and women ceased to rule together and sought independence rather than interdependence. Power struggles ensued with men seeking to dominate women and women seeking to be liberated from male authority. Such was the condition of the Corinthian Church which warranted a strong correction from the Apostle Paul. [5] Consequently, in a male dominant world, theologies began to be forged interpreting the worth and value of women based upon the *"fallen" model of Eve* rather than upon God's original plan. Thus, even within the Church, the concept developed that women were inferior and must unconditionally submit to the rule of men.

1-(Gen. 3:8-13); 2-(Gen. 3:16); 3-(Judges 19:22-29); 4-Gen. 4:23; 1 Kings 11:1-3; Matt. 19:8); 5-(1 Cor. 11:2-12).

3. Men and women after redemption (the "redeemed" model):

a. The Intent of Redemption

Redemption is God's plan for correcting all that Satan and sin have corrupted—restoring men and women back to their original purpose in God. Consequently, the failure of theology to properly portray the roles of men and women slows (and in some instances stops) the fullness of God's work on earth. Scripture clearly teaches that all discriminatory barriers which have wrongfully caused separations between the races and genders have been dealt with through the Atonement. [1] *Thus, men and women are reunited through redemption to their original mission as <u>co-rulers</u> over the earth.*

1-(Rom. 10:12; Gal. 3:26-29; Col. 3:9-15).

b. The Structure of Male Headship

The admonition of Paul to Timothy concerning women was not intended to be an ecclesiastical doctrine limiting the potential of women. [1] He was simply correcting a fallen tendency in women to function apart from and even in opposition to men. (Likewise, Paul addresses fallen tendencies in men that also must be corrected. [2]) Knowing the deep-rooted nature of sin and the life-long process of redemption, Paul set a godly structure over the authority struggles between men and women bringing stability to both the Church and the home. Accordingly, men are charged to *exercise godly responsibility* (not dominant authority) over the woman even as Christ loves the Church. Women are instructed to *respect and submit to Christ-like authority* in men. [3] Just as the law served as a "schoolmaster" to lead us to mature freedom in Christ,[4] even so this relationship structure serves to guide men and women to the maturity of God's intention—ministering together, without competition or contention, for the common goal of fulfilling their divine mission. [5] Thus, this structure provides an orderly framework for honoring headship and accomplishing God's purposes on earth.

1-(1 Tim. 2:9-15); 2-(Eph. 5:25-31; Col. 3:19, 21); 3-(1 Cor. 11:3-10; Eph. 5:22-33); 4-(Gal. 3:24-29); 5-(1 Cor. 11:11-12; Eph. 5:21; Gal. 5:13-15).

c. Women in Leadership

In his other Scriptural writings, the Apostle Paul gives truth that brings additional clarity to the issue of women in ministry. He included women in his discussion of Elders and Deacons concerning their qualifications for leadership in the Church. [1] He commended many women who were diligent workers for the cause of Christ. [2] One in particular served as a deaconess (diakonon—feminine) in the church at Cenchrea.[3] Paul specifically recognized Aquila and Priscilla as a prominent husband and wife team who ministered as a couple. [4] He even speaks of the glory (the splendor) that is produced when men and women function together according to God's design. [5] As a result of redemption, men and women are no longer independent of one another but are subject to the gift of God in each other. [6] Therefore, when this Biblical principle is applied to God's Church, it becomes evident that the ministries of both men and women must be included in the leadership of the Church—each bringing their own gifts as co-laborers to represent the full counsel of God.

1-(1 Tim. 3:11); 2-(Phil. 1-2; Rom. 16:6-15); 3-(Rom. 16:1-2); 4-(1 Cor. 16:19; Rom. 16:3-4); 5-(1 Cor. 11:7-10; Eph. 5:22-33); 6-(1 Cor. 11:11-12; Eph. 5:21).

d. Redeemed Attitudes

With an honest assessment of Biblical truth, it becomes necessary for both men and women to "lay aside" fallen attitudes and allow their paradigm to be renewed according to God's original design. [1] One who earnestly seeks truth will confess (along with Peter) that God is not a "respecter of persons". He does not discriminate! [2] In the spirit of redemptive truth, God anoints and distributes gifts to whom <u>He will</u>—not according to gender. [3] Thus old prejudices must give way to the acceptance that women are also recipients of the gifts described in Rom 12, 1 Cor. 12, and Eph. 4. Furthermore, it is incumbent upon God's Church to recognize, honor and release gifts of ministry and leadership in women as well as in men. *In the final analysis, submission is not on the basis of one who is "inferior" or "superior." It is according to the God-given gift and anointing in an individual and not according to his or her gender.*

1-(Eph. 4:22-25); 2-(Acts 10:34); 3-(1 Cor. 12:11-27).

IX. THE MINISTRIES AND PRACTICES OF THE CHURCH

A. Of the Sacraments of the Church

The Sacraments of the Church are those holy ordinances instituted and appointed by Christ Himself as signs and seals of the covenant between God and His people. A sacrament is a visible and sensible sign that holds the sacred mystery (sacramentum) of a deeper reality in which the grace of God and the benefits of covenant are represented, sealed and applied to the believer by the real presence of Christ. The Sacraments are not optional for the believer but are necessary elements of the covenantal relationship between God and man. The Sacraments are inseparable from redemption, not by virtue of the physical elements themselves, but by the blessing of Christ and the working of His Spirit in the believer who receives them by faith. The two great sacraments of the Christian Church are:

1. Water Baptism:

According to Scripture, believers must enter by faith into the sacrament of Water Baptism in order to be spiritually united with Christ and receive the redemptive benefits of His death and His resurrection. [1] Through Water Baptism, believers experience a "spiritual circumcision" of the heart (circumcision being the sign of the Old Testament Covenant with God [2]) which is necessary if they are to enter into the New Testament Covenant relationship with Christ. [3] As a result, believers are adopted as God's children; they become true members of His Body (the Church), and they are heirs of His Kingdom. [4] Hence, Water Baptism is a one-time event in the Christian's life so closely related to salvation that it does not need to be repeated. Accordingly, we practice a "Believers Baptism" [5] meaning that infants and children who are not old enough to make a personal decision for Christ are Dedicated to the Lord rather than baptized. Thus they are brought into the Covenant of their parents until they become responsible and accountable before God to make an individual commitment to Christ and receive salvation. As to a specific mode of baptism (immersion, sprinkling or pouring), Scripture does not make this an issue, only that one must be a believer in Christ and place his/her faith in His atoning work. [6] Finally, in Water Baptism all three Persons of the Godhead are so intricately involved in this mystical work that Jesus specifically instructed His disciples to baptize in the name of the Father, Son and Holy Spirit.[7] The essential nature of the sacrament is clearly evident in Christ's mandate requiring Water Baptism to be an inseparable element of the work of the Church in fulfilling the Great Commission of preaching the Gospel all the world. [8]

1-(Acts 2:38; Rom. 6:3-10; 1 Peter 3:21); 2-(Gen. 17:10-11; Deut. 10:16); 3-(Rom. 2:28-29; Col. 2:11-14; Gen. 17:10-11); 4-(Rom. 8:15-17; Gal. 4:4-7); 5-(Mark 16:16; Acts 16:30-33); 6-(Acts 8:36-38; 16:30-33; 19:4-5); 7-(Matt. 28:19); 8-(Matt. 28:19-20; Mark 16:15-16).

2. The Lord's Supper:

The significance of the Lord's Supper (also called the "Eucharist" and "Communion") is foreshadowed in the

Passover meal when Israel was delivered from the bondage of Egypt. Upon seeing the blood of the sacrificial lamb applied to the houses of the Israelites, the Lord "passed over" their households and delivered them from the plague of death.[1] When Christ, the sacrificial Lamb of God, was slain on the cross, His sacrificed body and blood was spiritually applied to the lives of those who believe in His atoning work. Accordingly, God "passes over" their sins and delivers them from spiritual death. The mystery of this sacrament is that the broken body and shed blood of our Lord is spiritually present and redemptively applied through Covenant to those who, in faith, partake of the physical elements of bread and wine. Thus great thanksgiving (literally "Eucharist") surrounds believers who receive the Lord's Supper for it is through this New Covenant in Christ's blood, that sins are forgiven (based upon His work alone) and an eschatological promise is given of His return.[2] Partaking of the Body and Blood of the Lord is not optional in the Christian faith. According to the very words of Jesus, "unless you eat the flesh of the Son of Man and drink His blood, you have no life in yourselves".[3] And the Table of the Lord is far more than a memorial to Christ; it is the spiritual sharing and consuming of His real presence which gives the believer full assurance of resurrection from the dead and eternal life.[4] The Bible gives a very strong warning that the Lord's Supper is intended only for those who are true believers and who understand the spiritual significance of this sacrament. Consequently, participants are required to examine and correct their own spiritual relationship with Christ and His Body (the Church) as they partake of the Table of the Lord.[5]

1-(Ex. 12:3-14); 2-(Matt. 26:26-28; 1 Cor. 11:23-26); 3-(John 6:53); 4-(John 6:54-58); 5-(1 Cor. 11:27-32).

B. Of the Ordinances and Practices of the Church

The Ordinances of the Church are solemn ecclesiastical rites performed within the Biblical authority of Christ's Church signifying the pronouncement of spiritual blessings and the impartation of God's grace according to the need and nature of the ordinance. These ordinances of the Church include:

1. The Blessing and Consecration of the Covenant of Marriage:

Christian marriage is the joining together of a man and a woman in a sacred Covenant between themelves and God. [1] Since it was God who originally created man and woman and inseparably joined them together, [2] He is obviously the Author and Sustainer of marriage. The Covenant of marriage under God's authority synergistically joins the man (the masculine image of God) and the woman (the feminine image of God) into a collective expression of God's character that is necessary if their union is to effectively accomplish God's will on earth. [3] A Christian Marriage is intended to produce the witness of a Christ-centered household that reflects God's structure of headship and submission to godly authority. [4] Resident within the family unit that is blessed of God is an environment of love and trust, [5] faithful companionship [6] and the provision for nurturing and training children for the work of the Lord.[7] In addition, a Christian Marriage is intended to be an earthly witness of the spiritual relationship between Christ (The Husband) and His Church (The Bride).[8] In order for a such a marriage to express all that is intended by God, the Church presides over the marriage ceremony, proclaims God's intentions, pronounces God's blessing over that union and consecrates the husband and wife to be God's witness to the world as a Christian married couple.

1-(Mal. 2:14); 2-(Gen. 2:18-24; Matt. 19:4-6); 3-(Gen. 1:26-28); 4-(1 Cor. 11:3; Eph. 5:22-24); 5-(Eph. 5:25; Col. 3:18); 6-(Gen. 2:18, 21-24); 7-(Ps. 127:3-5; Prov. 22:6; Eph. 6:1-4; Col. 3:20-21); 8-(Eph. 5:22-32).

2. The Blessing and Dedication of Children:

Within God's creative plan for men and women, He provided for the procreation of children and commanded them to multiply and fill the earth. [1] Children raised and trained under parental authority submitted to Christ become part of God's plan for assuring that a witness of His rule and reign continues to be expressed on the earth.[2] As a result of this, children become a potential threat to satanic forces who have not only rebelled against God but who also plot to destroy His witnesses on earth.[3] Therefore, it is imperative that children, even as infants, are presented to the Lord and brought into the provisions and protection of their parents' Covenant with God.[4] The Church, as God's embassy on earth, [5] dedicates these children to the Lord, pronounces God's blessings over them [6] and confirms the Covenant of their parents for the faithful raising and training of their children to serve God.[7] Such children are included in their family's Covenant until they become responsible and accountable before God to accept Christ as their Savior and enter into Water Baptism and their own personal Covenant with Him.

1-(Gen. 1:26-28; 9:1,7); 2-(Gen. 3:15; 18:19; 22:17-18; Ps. 127:3-5); 3-(Ex. 1:15-22; Matt. 2:13-16; John 10:10); 4-(Luke 18:15-17; 1 Cor. 7:14); 5-(2 Cor. 5:20); 6-(Matt. 19:13-15; Mark 10:13-16; Luke 2:34); 7-(Deut. 6:5-9; Prov. 22:6; Eph. 6:1-4; Col. 3:20-21).

3. Prayers of Dedication:

Although God's people are the objects of His love and recipients of His blessings, it is in keeping with the Biblical pattern to dedicate physical buildings, facilities, and artifacts for the purposes of ministry and to the service of the Lord. God visibly demonstrated His approval at the completion of the tabernacle in the wilderness by filling it with His glory.[1] Prayers and sacrifices were offered in dedicating the great Temple of Solomon to God. [2] And the wall of Jerusalem was dedicated to God with great gladness, hymns of thanksgiving, songs and joyful celebrations. [3] In the New Testament, the Disciples were authorized by Jesus to either pronounce or retract blessings upon households and cities depending upon their receptiveness to the messengers of the Lord.[4] The Church, therefore, presides over and makes dedicatory prayers for buildings, facilities, homes or artifacts that are devoted to the ministry or work of the Lord.

1-(Ex. 40:33-34); 2-(2 Chr. 6:10-13, 18-21, 40; 7:4-10); 3-(Neh. 12:27-31; 43,45); 4-(Matt. 10:5-16).

4. The Laying on of Hands:

The Laying on of Hands by the Elders of the Church is a physical act that signifies the spiritual impartation of blessings, gifts, anointing, or other necessary qualities to another person as needed for a higher dimension of service to the Lord. According to the Biblical pattern, the laying of hands is used for imparting a prophetic blessing, [1] consecrating leadership, [2] imparting spiritual gifts, [3] healing the sick, [4] blessing and dedication of children,[5] and ordaining and sending forth ministry. [6] The laying on of hands is not an act of human desire nor is it to be performed hastily. [7] This must be done at the inspiration of God and according to the witness of the Holy Spirit, who imparts His gifts and gives His anointing, as He desires. [8]

1-(Gen. 48:13-20); 2-(Num. 27:22; Acts 6:1-6); 3-(Deut. 34:9; Acts 8:17-18; 19:6; 1 Tim. 4:14; 2 Tim. 1:6); 4-(Mark. 6:5; Luke 13:13; Acts. 28:8; James 5:13-15); 5-(Mark 10:13-16); 6-(Acts 13:1-3; 1 Tim. 4:14); 7-(1 Tim. 5:22); 8-(1 Cor. 12:11, 18).

5. The Consecration and Ordination of Church Leadership:

The offices held by Church leadership are sacred offices of trust and responsibility that require personal consecration and a special anointing from God in order to properly carry out their duties. The charge upon Church leadership is a holy charge of God [1] to lead and care for His people in the example of Christ Himself. [2]

1-(1 Tim. 5:21; 6:13-16; 2 Tim. 4:1-2); 2-(1 Tim. 4:12; Titus 2:7-8; 1 Pet. 5:1-5).

a. The Offices of the Ordained Ministry:

The calling of an individual to the Ordained Ministry (the Five-fold/Ascension Gift Ministries) is the work of Christ who is the Head of the Church.[1] It is incumbent upon the Church to make certain that the gifts and anointing for ministry are resident within the individual prior to ordination since these offices are not to be committed to weak or incapable persons.[2] The Consecration of a person to the Ordained Ministry is an act of the Presbytery of the Church acknowledging the call of Christ upon that person accompanied by prayer, the laying on of hands and, when appropriate, a prophetic word from the Lord.[3] By this act, an individual is publicly set forth, authorized and commissioned to proclaim the Word, administer the Sacraments, promote the unity of the Church as the Body of Christ, and guide and nurture the Christian community toward God's purposes for their lives.

1-(Eph. 4:7, 10-16); 2-(1 Tim. 3:6-7, 10; 5:22); 3-(1 Tim. 4:14; 2 Tim. 1:6).

b. The Offices of Support Ministry:

The Diaconate and other support ministries are set forth in the Church to assist the Ordained Ministry in caring for the people and in conducting the work of the Lord.[1] The qualifications for those who assist in ministry are clearly spelled out in Scripture in order that only men and women of godly character be installed in these offices.[2] Deacons and other support ministers are publicly set in office by the laying on of hands and prayer by the Presbytery of the Church.[3] Thus they are duly charged and set forth to assist in caring for the people and to perform their duties with compassion and diligence as unto the Lord.

1-(Ex. 18:21-22; Num. 3:5-9; Acts 6:1-6); 2-(Ex. 18:21; Acts 6:3; 1 Tim. 1-13; Titus 1:5-8); 3-(Acts 6:5-6)

6. Reconciliation of the Penitent:

Reconciliation is the work of God whereby a hostile world, alienated and estranged from God by rebellion, is reconciled back to Him through the Substitutionary Atonement of His own Son. [1] Through reconciliation, man is restored to his former state of peace and harmony with God and with his fellow man. [2] The overriding purpose of reconciliation, aside from manifesting the merciful grace of God, is to restore fallen man to his original assignment of representing God's Kingdom on earth and witnessing against satanic rule.[3] Reconciliation for the sinner is realized when the Holy Spirit applies Christ's work of redemption to the repentant soul who recognizes his sins, expresses deep godly sorrow and consciously turns from sin toward God's grace and forgiveness. [4] Repentance produces a desire within the sinner to confess and forsake his sins and proclaim Christ to be both his Savior and his Lord. [5] Christ, the Mediator of our salvation, has made His Church the ambassadors of His Kingdom and has given her the ministry of reconciliation—entreating the world to be reconciled to God. [6] Therefore, the Church, when receiving a confession made by a penitent sinner, proclaims that his sins are forgiven based upon the applied redemptive work of Christ and declares that he is released from the guilt of sin and reconciled back to God. [7] Furthermore, as a tangible demonstration of the reality of reconciliation, the Church restores that person into full fellowship and service to the Lord within the congregation.[8]

1-(Rom. 5:8-11; Col. 1:19-22); 2-(Eph. 2:12-22); 3-(Gen. 1:26-28; Ps. 8:3-6; Mal. 4:3; Rom. 16:20); 4-(Ps. 51:3-4; 2 Cor. 7:10; Acts 26:18); 5-(1 John 1:9; Rom. 10:9-10); 6-(2 Cor. 5:18-20); 7-

(John 20:22; Luke 4:18-19; James 5:17); 8-(Gal. 6:1-3; 2 Cor. 2:6-8).

7. Prayers for the Sick:

Ever since sin entered the human race through Adam's transgression, man has been under the curse of physical pain, suffering, disease and ultimately death.[1] In view of God's eternal purpose to correct and restore all that is corrupt in His universe, He provides the availability of divine healing for the sick and protection from disease for His Covenant people.[2] In addition to being an expression of God's compassion toward suffering humanity,[3] divine healing is a foretaste of the Kingdom of God and a demonstration of His authority over sin, disease and evil spirits that cause sickness. [4] Thus God is glorified for His authority and work of grace, and His people are restored to serve Him in strength and health.[5] It is key to understand, at this point, that God has chosen to work through His Church to demonstrate the benefits of His Kingdom and to accomplish His will on earth. Therefore, Christ commissioned His Church to represent His compassion and authority on the earth by visiting the sick, [6] praying over them, anointing them with oil [7] and proclaiming their healing according to the provisions of the Kingdom of God. [8] God graciously and compassionately responds to all prayers offered in faith, [9] but ultimately it is God and not the Church who heals and determines the final outcome of all prayers for healing according to His higher purposes. [10]

1-(Gen. 2:17; 3:16-19); 2-(Ex. 15:26; 23:25); 3-(Matt. 14:14; Mark 1:40-42); 4-(Luke 5:17-26; 13:11-13); 5-(Matt. 8:14-15; 15:31; 20:34); 6-(Matt. 25:43-46); 7-(James 5:14-16); 8-(Matt. 10:1, 7-

8; Mark 16:15-18); 9-(James 5:15; Matt. 9:22, 28-29); 10-(John 11:4; 2 Cor. 12:7-10; Philip. 1:19-24).

8. The Discipline of Prayer and Fasting:

In the history of the Old Testament, the first mention of fasting food and water was with Moses. This was done at a time of great consecration on the Mountain of God when he received the Covenant of the Ten Commandments directly from the Lord.[1] Again Moses repeated his fast as he grieved over the sin of Israel and feared the consequences of God's judgment.[2] In other instances, believers made supplications and humbled themselves before God with prayers of contrition, fasting and the wearing of sackcloth and ashes in times of tragedy or great need. [3] In addition to individual fasts, corporate fasts of God's people were called on special occasions such as the Day of Atonement and at times of national distress or calamity.[4] Though God honored those who humbled themselves in this way, [5] He nevertheless strongly admonished the Israelites that their fasts had degenerated into religious facades while they continued to live wickedly. [6] Jesus addressed the issue of fasting in a similar way, correcting shallow religious displays of self-righteous hypocrisy. [7] Yet, Jesus gave even greater insight by revealing that when faith is coupled with prayer and fasting, it produces power and authority to overcome demonic forces. [8] The practice of prayer and fasting continued in the New Testament during times of special dedication and seeking the Lord for the work of the Church in the world. [9] In summary, fasting, when accompanied with prayers and faith, is a legitimate Biblical practice among God's people. Fasting is a sign of the inner attitude of the heart when a person is willing to deny the pleasures of the flesh in special times of submission and consecration to God and for the advancement of His cause on earth. The discipline of fasting strengthens prayer (in terms of personal commitment, not a "magical" religious formula) and prepares one to hear from God concerning the matter at hand. In the present-day Church, methods of fasting may vary from the abstinence of full meals to a fast of certain types of enjoyable foods or perhaps pleasant activities. The duration of fasts may be for a day or more, or it may involve the missing of several meals each week for a season of time. Though methods may vary, the important issue is the motive of the heart as a believer takes authority and dominion over his own flesh and enters into a time of prayer and consecration to hear from God.

1-(Ex. 34:28); 2-(Deut. 9:18-20); 3-(Judges 20:26-27; 2 Sam. 12:15-23; Ps. 35:12; Dan. 9:2-19); 4-(Lev. 23:27-32; 2 Chr. 29:1-13); 5-(Judges 20:28; Dan. 9:20-23; 2 Chr. 20:14-15); 6-(Is. 58:1-5; Jer. 14:10-12); 7-(Matt. 6:16-18); 8-(Matt. 17:18-21); 9-(Acts 13:1-3; 14:21-23).

9. Ministry to the Dying:

Physical death is the most final of all earthly events that will occur in the life of a human being. Physical death is that point of irreversible separation in which the human spirit and soul leave the body [1] and return to God for judgment.[2] The body then dies and returns to the earth from which it came.[3] Not only is death physically irreversible, but even more crucial, it is that point of eternal determination where the spiritual condition of the person is forever sealed.[4] Knowing this, the Church has an essential ministry to both the dying and to those who are left behind. For the dying sinner, there is no ministry greater than sharing the Gospel of God's grace and giving one final opportunity to escape eternal death and hell by receiving salvation through Christ.[5] For the believer who is dying, it is a time of building faith and confidence in the Savior, dispelling all fear of death [6] and trusting in God to transport him safely to His heavenly kingdom. [7] Then, when the moment of death is imminent, the Church has the authority to assist the believer in committing and releasing his spirit and soul back to the Lord.[8] For the grieving loved ones who are in the Lord, the Church ministers comfort and hope [9] knowing that the departed saint will be with the Lord forever and that there will be a great reunion when all the saints are resurrected at His return. [10]

1-(Gen. 35:18; John 19:30); 2-(Eccles. 12:7; Heb. 9:27); 3-(Gen. 3:19; James 2:26); 4-(Luke 16:22-31; Rev. 22:11-12); 5-(Luke 23:42-43; James 5:19-20; Jude 22-23); 6-(Luke 12:4-5; 1 Cor. 15:54-55); 7-(Ps. 116:15; 2 Tim. 4:6-8, 18); 8-(Ps. 31:5; Luke 23:46; Acts 7:59-60); 9-(2 Sam. 12:23; James 1:27); 10-(1 Thess. 4:13-18; 1 Cor. 15:42-44).

C. Of the Responsibility of Believers

God created men and women as free moral agents who are personally responsible and morally accountable for their own decisions, choices and actions. Even though the work of salvation is purely the work of God's grace toward sinners, He nevertheless sets human response as the condition by which His grace becomes effective in people's lives. Consequently, God will not make decisions for people. Instead He communicates His will, precepts and rules for life and allows people to freely choose to obey or to defy

His will. Christians, therefore, are personally responsible before God in the following areas of their own lives:

1. Believers are responsible for spiritual growth in their own lives.

Having responded to the saving grace of God and knowing that the Holy Spirit is enabling and working in His people, believers are nevertheless responsible to "work out" the details of their salvation [1] even as they are being conformed to the image of Christ. This "working out" process of salvation most certainly includes the responsibility of each Christian to come to know Christ in an ever-growing, personal and intimate relationship.[2] Believers are required to deliberately lay aside the corruption of the "old self" and put on the "new self" that is recreated in the likeness of God. [3] This process of salvation includes purposely walking according to the Spirit rather than the flesh [4] and adding godly character to their lives, which brings certainty of salvation. [5] God requires Christians to diligently study Scripture and lay a foundation of Biblical truth and experience upon which the rest of their lives can be built. [6] Finally, believers "work out" their salvation by pressing on to maturity and spiritually growing in the things concerning Christ.[7] God calls all believers into a "spiritual priesthood" wherein they are required to obey the voice of God and keep His covenant, [8] to offer up spiritual sacrifices of doing good for others and praise unto God,[9] and to devote themselves to prayer and thanksgiving. [10] However, the "priesthood of believers" should not be interpreted as believers independent from the structure of God's Church. On the contrary, they are required by God to maintain relationship and obedience to those over them in the Lord. [11]

1-(Philip. 2:12-13); 2-(Philip. 3:8-10; 1 John 2:3-6); 3-(Eph. 4:17-32); 4-(Gal. 5:16-26); 5-(2 Pet. 1:3-11); 6-(2 Tim. 2:15; 3:16-17); 7-(Eph. 4:13-16; Heb. 5:14-6:2); 8-(Heb. 19:5-6); 9-(1 Pet. 2:1-10; Heb. 13:15-16); 10-(Col. 4:2-3; Philip. 4:4-7); 11-(Eph. 4:11-16; 1 Thess. 5:12-13; Heb. 13:7,17).

2. Believers are responsible to use their spiritual gifts in ministering to others.

Once people receive salvation and are transferred into the Kingdom of Christ, they are responsible to present themselves as living and holy sacrifices to serve the Lord according to the grace He has given them and the specific gifts they have received from God. [1] God gives both natural and spiritual gifts to His people, not for personal benefit or gain, but for ministering to one another [2] and for contributing to the common good of the whole Church.[3] Proper stewardship and effective use of God-given gifts and abilities is a very serious issue with God. According to the very words of Christ (the King Himself), every person will be personally accountable to Him for the use of these gifts in helping others, regardless of their abilities. [4] Furthermore, those who are faithful in their gifts will be rewarded greatly, but those who have foolishly wasted or abused theirs will lose their reward, with some even being severely punished. [5]

1-(Rom. 12:1-8); 2-(1 Pet. 4:10-11); 3-(1 Cor. 12:1-11; 2 Cor. 14:12,26); 4-(Matt. 25:14-46); 5-(Matt. 24:45-51; 1 Cor. 3:13-15).

3. Believers are responsible for the Truth that they have received.

Scripture tells us that the light of God's truth has come into the world and that all men are judged in accordance to their response to this Light.[1] God holds every human being accountable for even the most elementary truth of His self-revelation that is evident in creation. [2] How much more, therefore, will God hold accountable those who know His will and His ways yet deliberately disobey. [3] Herein is a great truth: God justly judges all men according to the level of revelation that is made known to them. [4] For those who have returned to their evil practices even after being delivered, it would have been better for them not to have known the truth than to have known it and turned away. [5] Furthermore, teachers of God's truth, who have received revelation and are trusted to be stewards of His mysteries, will be judged even more severely if they do not practice the truth that they teach. [6]

1-(John 3:19-21; 1 John 1:5-8); 2-(Rom. 1:18-23); 3-(James 4:17); 4-(Luke 12:47-48); 5-(2 Pet. 2:20-22); 6-(1 Cor. 4:1-2; James 3:1).

4. Believers are responsible over the natural affairs of life.

Although Christians are spiritual creatures born of God, they are also natural human beings who live in the reality of a time/space world with natural needs, desires and choices to make. Even though believers enjoy a special covenant relationship and a divine destiny in God, He nevertheless requires of them, along with the rest of the world, to make responsible life decisions and become productive members of society. Furthermore, since man was created and crowned by God from the very beginning to be ruler over the lower creation, [1] how much more should he be able to rule his own life according to the purposes of God. What a tragedy it would be if God's own people, who have available to them the Word and wisdom of God, [2] fail in their witness to the world as proper administrators of even the natural affairs of their own lives. [3] Hence, Christians are responsible over such natural areas as: choosing godly friends, [4] choosing godly husbands and wives [5] and caring for their families according to God's standards. [6] In addition, believers must be faithful stewards over their finances, [7] have good work ethics [8] and make sound business decisions.[9] God's people are required by the Lord Himself to be in subjection to civil authorities [10] and to even be good stewards over the earth. [11] Finally, since God gives to all people the authority to rule their own lives, the Church should never attempt to usurp that right or make decisions for them. The role of the Church is to proclaim the truth of God's will and His ways then allow each person or each family to choose for themselves. [12]

1-(Ps. 8:5-8); 2-(2 Tim. 3:15-17; 2 Pet. 1:2-4); 3-(1 Tim. 3:4-7); 4-(Prov. 3:30; 1 Cor. 15:33); 5-(Prov. 18:22; 2 Cor. 6:14-17; Eph. 5:22-33); 6-(Gen. 18:19; 1 Tim. 3:5; 5:8); 7-(Luke 16:10-13); 8-(Prov. 31:13-15; 2 Thess. 3:10-12); 9-(Prov. 11:15; 27:23-27; 31:16); 10-(Rom. 13:1-7); 11-(Gen. 2:15; Rev. 11:18 b); 12-(Deut. 30:19-20; Josh. 24:14-15).

D. Of the Ministries of the Church

1. The Ministry unto God of Praise and Worship:

The first and foremost of all the commandments is to love God with all your heart, soul, mind, and strength. [1] For the committed Christian, this means that the full spectrum of human energies must be dedicated to the devotion, reverence, adoration and service of the Lord. Praise is the exuberant expression of a grateful heart with words of adoration, public rejoicing and songs honoring God for what He has done. [2] Worship, in the language of Scripture, conveys the idea of humbling oneself before an immensely more powerful [3] yet merciful Being whose gracious acts [4] evoke a life of total reverence, submission and service. True praise and worship are never artificially manufactured rituals but most certainly flow as genuine heartfelt responses to the manifest presence of Almighty God who is both our Creator and our Savior. [5] For the individual, worship is the response of one who comprehends the reality of God and understands the eternal work of salvation by which his soul has been gloriously redeemed from the power of sin and the devil. [6] Corporately, worship is the priestly ministry [7] of the Church whom God has made to be a kingdom of priests unto Him. [8] The spiritual significance of praise and worship is not only giving to God what is rightfully His, but also it becomes a testimony against the fallen angels who abandoned their original purpose in heaven. [9] Praise and worship in the Church may be expressed in many ways depending upon the mood and setting of a service. God's people praise and worship Him by instrumental music, [10] singing, [11] dancing, [12] lifting hands, [13] shouting, [14] clapping the hands, [15] times of silence, [16] sacrificially giving offerings and personal service, [17] and dramatic presentations recounting the mighty works of God. [18] The final result of glorifying God with praise and worship is enjoying the very presence of the living God—knowing that it pleases Him and that He seeks those who will worship Him in spirit and truth.[19]

1-(Deut. 6:5,13; Mark 12:29-30); 2-(2 Sam. 22:50-51; Ps. 106:1-2); 3-(Ps. 66:3-4; Jer. 32:27; Matt. 14:32-33); 4-(Ex. 12:27; 20:2; John 9:6-7,37-38); 5-(Ex. 34:5-8; Luke 24:31-32); 6-(John 4:24; Jude 24-25); 7-(Ex. 28:1; Neh. 12:44-45); 8-(Ex. 19:6; Rev. 1:6; 5:10); 9-(Ps. 148:1-5; Jude 6; Eph. 3:10; Rev. 4:8-11); 10-(Ps. 33:1-2;150:3); 11-(Ps. 92:1; 104:33; Col. 3:16); 12-(Ps. 149:3; 2 Sam. 6:14-15); 13-(Ps. 63:3-4; 134:2; 1 Tim. 2:8); 14-(Ps. 66:1-3; 71:23); 15-(Ps. 47:1); 16-(Hab. 2:20; Zech. 2:13); 17-(Gen. 22:5; Rom. 12:1); 18-(Ps. 106:1-48; Ex. 15:1-18); 19-(Ps. 22:3; John 4:23).

2. The Ministry of the Word of God:

The Bible is the Word of God in written form revealing His heart, mind and purposes to all mankind. Through the preaching, teaching, and exhortation of God's Word, there is a sacramental or mysterious working within human hearts whereby the Holy Spirit quickens and applies the truth and purposes of God to all who have united their faith with the Word. [1]

1-(Ps. 119:130; 1 Cor. 1:18; Heb. 4:1-2, 12).

a. Preaching:

Preaching is the proclamation or "crying forth" of God's Word through human vessels to all the world [1] concerning His will and purposes. Christ, who is the "Living Word", comes to men through the preached Word and produces both faith and spiritual life [2] in those who hear. Even as Christ preached the "Good News" of His coming Kingdom, [3] so also the Church is commissioned to preach His Word and to proclaim the rule of Christ (the Kingdom) to all the world. [4] Furthermore, when the Word of God is prophetically proclaimed by the unction of the Holy Spirit, [5] the creative force of the Word is released into the earth to execute His purposes, for "the Lord watches over His Word to perform it". [6]

1-(Mark 16:15; Acts 1:8); 2-(John 1:1, 14; Rom. 10:14-17); 3-(Matt. 4:17, 23; Luke 4:18-19, 43); 4-(Acts 10:40-42; 28:30-31; Matt. 24:14); 5-(Ezek. 37:4-10; Amos 3:7-8; Acts 2:17-21); 6-(Is. 55:11; Jer. 1:12).

b. Teaching:

The teaching of God's Word is the systematic presentation of Scriptural truth in clear and simplistic terms such that an understanding of God's will and purposes can be easily grasped and appropriated in human experience. Furthermore, those who teach in the Church are to pattern themselves after Jesus,[1] the Teacher. He taught His disciples through the demonstration of His life [2] concerning the true character and will of God [3] and His Kingdom. [4] The ultimate goal of teaching is to train believers to be mature and faithful disciples who will be equipped for the ministry and able to teach others as well.[5]

1-(1 Cor. 11:1; Eph. 5:1-2; 1 Pet. 2:21); 2-(John 14:8-12; Acts 1:1); 3-(Matt. 5; 6; 7); 4-(Matt. 13:1-53); 5-(Eph. 4:11-16; 2 Tim. 2:2; 3:16-17).

c. Exhortation:

Exhortation is boldly and persuasively speaking Scriptural truth [1] at the proper time to an individual or a group as prompted by the Holy Spirit. Exhortation holds the connotation of admonishing and warning [2] as well as entreating, encouraging and comforting.[3] As a ministry of the Word, exhortation has its perfect result when people are instructed and brought to the effectual awareness of God's grace and His loving correction [4] in order that they may know how to live in His Kingdom.[5]

1-(Titus 1:9); 2-(2 Tim, 4:2; Titus 2:15); 3-(1 Cor. 14:3; 1 Thess. 2:11; 1 Pet. 5:12); 4-(Heb. 12:5-6); 5-(1 Thess. 4:1-12).

3. The Ministry and Celebration of the Sacraments:

The Sacraments of the Church are holy ordinances instituted and appointed by the Lord Himself as signs and seals of His covenant with His people. For that reason, great care must be given to assure that they are administered in such a manner as to depict both the sacredness and the celebration of the occasion. According to the Scriptural pattern, the priesthood was ordained and set apart by the Lord to perform His work and minister God's covenantal ordinances to His people. [1] In keeping with this pattern and the tradition of the historic Church, only those who are duly set forth to the Ordained Ministry are authorized to minister the Sacraments of Water Baptism and the Lord's Supper. Consequently, the Sacraments are to be ministered with great reverence and in proper order, [2] yet with joyful celebration knowing that through them the grace of God and the benefits of covenant are mysteriously represented, sealed and applied to the believer by the real presence of Christ. It brings great joy to those who partake in faith, knowing that in Water Baptism they are raised up with Christ to walk in the newness of life and are adopted by God to become inheritors of His Kingdom. [3] Great thanksgiving ("Eucharist") also surrounds believers who receive the Lord's Supper realizing that, through the New Covenant in Christ's blood, sins are forgiven and a promise is made of the soon coming King in the fullness of His Kingdom. [4] Finally, believers celebrate the Sacraments with joy and expectation because of the spiritual sharing and consuming of Christ's real presence that gives full assurance of resurrection from the dead and eternal life. [5]

1-(Ex. 12:43; Jer. 33:18); 2-(1 Cor. 11:20-34); 3-(Rom. 6:3-10; 8:15-17); 4-(Matt. 26:26-28; I Cor. 11:23-26); 5-(John 6:53-58).

4. The Ministry of Equipping the Saints:

The ministry of equipping the Saints as set forth in Ephesians 4:7-16 is specifically the work of the Apostles, Prophets, Evangelists, Pastors and Teachers of the Church according to the gifts of Christ and includes the following:

a. Training Christians to Serve Others in Love:

"Equipping" the Saints conveys the idea of preparing believing men and women to serve others by knitting them together into a unified work force free of disputes or jealousy. [1] This includes helping them discover their gifts and callings as well as releasing them to function properly in the Body of Christ. As a result, Christians will work together using their spiritual gifts, [2] build up the Church in love, and become the mature Bride of Christ. [3] When the world sees a unified Church reaching out with love, then they will know that Christ is in the world today through His Church. [4]

1-(Luke 22:23-27); 2-(Rom. 12:1-8; 1 Cor. 12:1-31; 1 Pet. 4:8-10); 3-(Eph. 4:12, 15-16; 1 Thess. 5:11-14; Rev. 19:7); 4-(John 13:34-35; 17:21-23).

b. Teaching the Basics of the Faith:
"Unity of the Faith" requires a unified belief system of Scriptural truths concerning the Lord Jesus Christ and His work as the Son of God. [1] Through foundational Bible and catechism classes, the basics of the Christian faith are taught to the people, counteracting deceptive doctrines and heresies which may draw them astray or cause them to stumble. [2]

1-(Eph. 4:13; 2 Tim. 2:15; 3:16-17); 2-(Eph. 4:14; Titus 1:9; 2 Pet. 2:1).

c. Helping People to Become Mature and Discerning Christians:
Maturity requires a standard toward which growth is directed. The ultimate standard of maturity that the Church must focus upon is the character, obedience and mission of the Lord Jesus Christ. [1] Maturity is

progressively realized as Christians are taught to press beyond the elementary teachings of the Word, [2] deal effectively with their own flesh problems,[3] and grow in their discernment of the subtle workings of the forces of evil.[4]

1-(Rom. 8:29; Eph. 4:13, 15; 2 Pet. 3:18); 2-(Heb. 5:12-14; 6:1-2); 3-(Eph. 4:17-32); 4-(2 Cor. 11:3, 14; Eph. 4:14; Heb. 5:14).

5. The Ministry of Jesus Continued Through the Church (Pastoral Care):

Pastoral Care embodies the totality of the compassionate ministry of the Lord Jesus Christ as the "Good Shepherd" of His people. The Lord chose the imagery of a shepherd in both the Old and New Testaments to describe how He lovingly cares for His people. [1] Just as Jesus is the Chief Shepherd of His Church, likewise Pastors are His undershepherds, charged and fully accountable to care for the flock of God as He would Himself. [2] The spiritual significance of Pastors caring for their people goes beyond the work of natural oversight and becomes a demonstration of true servant leadership in God's Kingdom. [3]

1-(Ps. 23:1-6; John 10:11-15); 2-(Ezek. 34:1-16; Heb. 13:17; 1 Pet. 5:1-4); 3-(Mark 10:42-44; 1 Pet. 5:2- 3).

a. The Ministry and Work of a Shepherd:

As a shepherd, the Pastor cares for and ministers to God's people by leading them to spiritual provisions for their lives, guiding them in the way of righteousness and being with them in times of difficulty to express love, compassion, hope and comfort. [1] The shepherd protects God's people from harm and evil by warning them of the evil schemes of Satan and the pitfalls of life that could ruin their souls. [2] The Pastor who is truly a shepherd of God's people follows the example of Jesus in knowing the sheep, seeking the lost, freeing those who are held captive by sin and the devil, healing the broken hearted, and restoring men and women to their potential in Christ. [3]

1-(Ps. 23:1-4); 2-(Ps. 23:5-6; Ezek. 3:17-21; Eph. 6:11); 3-(Ezek. 34:1-16; Matt. 18:11-14; Luke 4:18-19).

b. The Practical Application of the Ministry of Jesus:

When the ministry of the Lord Jesus Christ is fully represented in His Church, it will be a proactive ministry of love and compassion, reaching out to bring hope, healing, wholeness and restoration. [1] In keeping with the character and mission of Jesus, the Church will develop ministries to release people from poverty, addictions, and oppressive circumstances of life. [2] The Church feeds the hungry, clothes and shelters the homeless, visits the sick and ministers to those in prison .[3] The Church cares for the orphans and widows, prays for the sick and gives godly wisdom to those who are seeking solutions for life's problems. [4] In summary, the Church ministers to the whole person in spirit, soul and body to restore and prepare God's people to reach their potential in Christ and become a living demonstration of God's Kingdom working on earth as it is in heaven. [5]

1-(Matt. 9:35-38); 2-(Luke 4:18-19); 3-(Matt. 25:34-40); 4-(James 1:27; 5:14-16; 3:13-18); 5-(1 Thess. 5:23-24; Matt. 6: 9-13).

6. The Ministry of Prayer:

Prayer (proseuchomai), in the language of the New Testament, reveals the understanding that God invites His people to "draw near" to Him and "speak" with Him about the concerns of their hearts. This gracious invitation allows mortal man to step beyond his veil of humanity into the realms of eternity, even into the very heart of God. It is from this vantage point of prayer that vision becomes clear, solutions are given, despair gives way to God's higher purposes, and God's peace that passes all understanding floods the soul.

a. Prayer is mutual Fellowship and Communion between man and God.

Although God is the awesome, all-powerful God of the universe, He is also a personal God who lovingly shares Himself and His will with His moral creatures. The evidence of God's desire for communion with man is seen throughout Scripture from the Garden as God "walked" and spoke with Adam and Eve [1] to the end of time when God again freely dwells among His people.[2] In prayer, deep calls unto deep, and the human spirit communes with God's Holy Spirit who brings wisdom and understanding. [3] It is in prayer that we "taste and see" the goodness of God and experience the refreshing fullness of joy that only comes from His presence. [4] In prayer, the believer ministers to the Lord with words and songs (of the mind and of the spirit) that bless their Lord and Savior. [5] It is also in prayer that the very "thoughts" of God [6] are made known. A spiritually intimate relationship between man and God is not only established, but flourishes and is melded into oneness of heart and purpose. [7]

1-(Gen. 3:8); 2-(Rev. 21:3-4); 3-(Ps. 42:7; Prov. 20:27; 1 Cor. 2:9-13); 4-(Ps. 34:7; 16:11); 5-(1 Cor. 14:2, 14-15); 6-(Ps. 139:17); 7-(John 17:21).

b. Prayer activates the fulfillment of God's eternal purposes through the Church.

In the sovereign counsel of the Triune God, He has chosen to make known the mystery of His will and demonstrate His eternal wisdom through His Church.[1] Accordingly, prayer is that essential and powerful instrument that activates the fulfillment of God's purposes as the Church prophetically proclaims God's intentions on the earth. [2] Specifically, the first and foremost prayer that Jesus taught His disciples was much more than just a petition to God; it was an imperative proclamation that the Kingdom of God (His rule and will) will most certainly come to earth as it is in heaven.[3] This has always been the purpose of God from the beginning when rebellion first broke out and Satan's evil forces were cast to the earth.[4] Hence, the Church, individually and corporately, announces the presence of God's rule on earth, asks for effectual doors of ministry to be opened, and prays for divine utterance and protection for those who boldly preach the Gospel of the Kingdom to all the nations.[5] Jesus, Himself, gave to His Church the "Keys of the Kingdom of Heaven" as a powerful weapon to war against the authority of hell. [6] Through the power of prayer, the Church resists the devil, binding the work of evil in the world and loosing people from the bondage of Satan that blinds their minds to the truth of the Gospel. [7] Furthermore, with the understanding that angels are agents of God's providential work toward humankind, the Church, as the co-worker of Christ on earth, can appeal to the Father for angelic assistance in time of great need. [8] Jesus, knowing the enormity of this global assignment, commanded His Church to pray for laborers to be sent into the harvest field of the world to work together in accomplishing the mission of the Church. [9] Finally, through the synergistic principle of "Agreement" in prayer, the Church can expect to see the power of prayer exponentially multiplied to bring to pass the effectual accomplishment of God's purposes on earth.[10]

1-(Amos 3:7; 1 Cor. 2:9-13; Eph. 1:9-11; 3:10); 2-(Is. 44:26; 55:11; Jer. 1:12); 3-(Matt. 6:9-10); -(Rev. 12:7-9; Hab. 2:14); 5-(Matt. 24:14; 2 Cor. 1:8-11; Eph. 6:18-20; 2 Thess. 3:1-2); 6-(Matt. 16:18-19); 7-(Eph. 6:10-20; James 4:7; 2 Cor. 4:3-4); 8-(2 Kings 6:15-18; Ps. 91:11-12; Matt. 26:53); 9-(Matt. 9:37-38; 1 Cor, 3:6-11); 10-(Matt. 18:19; Lev. 26:8; Deut. 32:30).

c. Prayer releases the provisions of heaven for personal and corporate needs.

As a gracious heavenly Father who has compassion on His children, God knows the frailty of human flesh and is attentive to the cry of His people for physical, emotional and spiritual needs. [1] Furthermore, God gives us the assurance that when we express our needs and requests to Him, with a thankful heart and in accordance with His will, He will hear from heaven and respond to the prayer offered in faith. [2] When praying believers establish the rule (Kingdom) of God as the first priority in their lives, they can expect to receive daily provisions, healing, forgiveness and deliverance from oppression and the powers of evil.[3] When His Church prays, God moves upon the hearts of governmental leaders to rule with fairness and justice.[4] Through the repentant prayer of God's people, He will forgive the sins of their nation and intervene to heal their land. [5] In praying for and encouraging one another, the Body of Christ will be built up in love and unity. [6] Prayers should be offered up for those around the world who are suffering and who are being persecuted for the cause of the Gospel .[7] Through the prayers of the leadership of the Church, God strengthens His people in their service to Him and fills them with the knowledge, wisdom and understanding necessary to accomplish their mission on earth.[8] Finally, the Church should most certainly pray for those who are deceived, lost and perishing in the world, that they may come to the saving grace of the Lord Jesus Christ. [9]

1-(Ps. 103:13-14; Ex. 3:7-8; Matt. 6:8); 2-(Philip. 4:6-7; 2 Chr. 7:14-16; 1 John 5:14-15); 3-(Matt. 6:11-15, 33; James 5:14-16); 4-(Prov. 21:1; 1 Tim. 2:1-2); 5-(2 Chr. 7:12-15); 6-(Col. 3:12-17; James 5:16); 7-(2 Cor. 4:8-11; Rev. 2:8-11); 8-(Col. 1:9-12); 9-(Rom. 9:1-5; 2 Cor. 4:3-4; 2 Pet. 3:9).

7. The Ministry of Outreach and Influence to the World:

a. Salt and Light to the World:

The early Church received her mission statement directly from the Head of the Church, the Lord Jesus Christ Himself. Jesus metaphorically described His Church as the *"Salt of the Earth"* and the *"Light of the World"* .[1] With the allegory of "Salt", Jesus was setting the course of the Church to be His "cleansing" and "preserving" agent in the world permeating and influencing society with the *"Leaven"* of the Kingdom of God. [2] As "Salt", the Church extends the cleansing power of the Blood of Christ [3] to the world and gives them the true "flavor" of God's character and purpose on earth.[4] The world must be "salted" with the compassionate works of Jesus ministering to the poor and bringing God's solutions to human suffering and oppression. [5] When Jesus spoke of His Church as "Light", He was indicating that He would send His Church into a world covered in spiritual darkness to reflect the "Light" of His goodness, righteousness and truth .[6] God, who causes light to shine out of darkness, [7] places His Church as "Light Bearers" in the midst of a crooked and perverse generation to appear as lights in a world that is groping in darkness. [8] Even as light exposes and makes things visible, so God's Church demonstrates (makes visible) through human experience the rule of Christ on earth, thus revealing the Kingdom of God and exposing Satan's evil kingdom.[9]

1-(Matt. 5:13-16); 2-(Matt. 13:33); 3-(Heb. 9:22); 4-(Col. 4:4-5; 2 Cor. 2:14-17); 5-(Matt. 9:35-38; Luke 4:18-19); 6-(Is. 60:1-

3; Eph. 5:8-10); 7-(Gen. 1:2-4; 2 Cor. 4:6); 8-(Philip. 2:15); 9-(Eph. 5:11-16).

b. Outreach to the World:

In His final prayer with His disciples, Jesus asked the Father to unify believers for their mission and to send them into the world as a demonstration of God's presence on earth. [1] The resurrected Christ, just before ascending back to heaven, charged His disciples to "go into all the world" to influence the nations with the rule of God. [2] Then as His final earthly act, Jesus sent the Holy Spirit to empower His Church as His witnesses both locally and even to the ends of the earth. [3] Thus the assignment of the Church is to go into all the world, bearing witness of the Christ as Lord and Savior and influencing all people with a demonstration of the Kingdom of God even as Jesus did in His earthly ministry. [4]

1-(John 17:15-23); 2-(Mark 16:15; Matt. 28:18-20); 3-(Acts 1:8; 2:1-11); 4-(Matt. 4:17; 10:7-8).

c. The Final Conclusion of Outreach and Influence:

The Church of the Lord Jesus Christ, as "Salt" and "Light", is destined by divine commission to enter into and influence every "kingdom" of society that has been corrupted by Satan's evil kingdom. [1] Accordingly, the "sons of the Kingdom" are God's good seed planted in the field of the world. They reflect the "Light" of God [2] as His witnesses within the world kingdoms of: government, commerce, finances, medicine, media, sports, education, arts, religion and private life. The Church, therefore, becomes the "conscience" of society speaking morally and ethically into each kingdom and bringing people to the awareness of God. [3] By strategically influencing heads of nations and governments for God, the "Leaven" of the rule of Christ will spread throughout all the nations thus fulfilling the Great Commission of the Church. [4] Furthermore, the Church becomes a model of the Kingdom of God (how God does things) in the world to ease human suffering and improve the quality of life for all people. [5] At last, when all the kingdoms of the world have received a witness of God's Kingdom sufficient for judgment, [6] then Christ will return to complete His work as King of His Kingdom, delivering it back to the Father as it was before Satan ever rebelled. [7]

1-(1 Cor. 9:19-23); 2-(Matt. 13:37-43); 3-(1 Kings 18:17-18; Dan. 2:27-28; Matt. 14:3-5); 4-(Matt. 13:33; 28:19-20); 5-(Matt. 9:35-38; Luke 4:18-19); 6-(John 3:17-21); 7-(Dan. 7:13-14; 1 Cor. 15:24; Rev. 11:15).

8. The Ministry of Restoration:

Restoration, in the language of the Old and New Testaments, expresses the idea of returning something or someone to its original purpose and to the original owner. It can also mean reversing a destructive situation or repairing that which is broken to function as originally designed. In addition, it carries the understanding of setting or arranging a government in proper order under the rightful rule of a king.

a. Restoration has its origin in God.

To fully understand the Ministry of Restoration in

the Church, the panoramic overview must be seen of the present corruption of the world, how it came to be, and God's plan to return it to His original purpose. Chaos, sin and disorder came to the earth from Lucifer's (Satan) insurrection and expulsion from heaven thus bringing the corruption of his evil kingdom to the physical world. [1] God, according to His eternal foreknowledge and purposes, decreed to ultimately destroy the curse of evil and restore all things back to the order and control of His eternal kingdom and to the glory of His righteous rule. [2] Thereupon God began His work of Restoration by the work of His Spirit—hovering over a chaotic and spiritually dark world, transforming disorder into order by the Word of God, and overcoming darkness with light. [3] It is the intention of God to restore mankind, the earth and even the entire universe (seen and unseen) back to His rightful rule.

1-(Is. 14:17; 45:18; Gen. 1:2; Jer. 4:23); 2-(Num. 14:21; Rom. 14:11; 2 Pet. 3:13; Rev. 22:3); 3-(Gen. 1:2-25; Heb. 11:3; John 1:1-5; 3:19).

b. Restoration was man's original assignment.

As God continued to unfold His plan of Restoration, He created man and set him as king of the lower creation with a mandate to multiply, fill, subdue and rule over all that was on the earth.[1] The obvious intention of God, since there was no hostility in the animal world prior to the fall, [2] was that man (by virtue of his likeness to God [3]) should represent God's righteous rule on a spiritually hostile planet and guard (Heb: "shamar") the Garden from intrusion of evil. [4] His assignment was to war against satanic forces and bring the earth back under the subjection of God's rule.[5]

1-(Gen. 1:26-28; Ps. 8:4-8); 2-(Gen. 9:2-3); 3-(Gen. 5:1); 4-(Gen. 2:15); 5-(Gen. 3:15; Mal. 4:3)

c. As recipients of Restoration, the assignment of the Church is to bring Restoration to all people. Since all have sinned and fallen short of their glorious assignment to represent God's righteous rule on earth, all men need the redemptive grace of God through Christ. [1] In the infinite wisdom of God (beyond the reasoning of natural man), God has chosen to restore fallen man from the degradation of sin and deposit in earthen vessels His heavenly treasure as a demonstration of His superior grace and power. [2] With the image and likeness of God being renewed, the Lord has also renewed man's original assignment and has given the Church the "Ministry of Reconciliation" as ambassadors of His Kingdom to the world.[3] Following the example of Christ, the Head of His Church, we reach out to restore the physical, emotional and spiritual needs of the poor, the oppressed and the outcasts of society, returning them to the human dignity that God intended. [4] Furthermore, the Church reaches out to all people who are in sin, regardless of their wrongdoing or the depths of their despair, [5] with the good news of repentance and restoration in Christ without bringing condemnation or guilt.[6] According to the Biblical meaning of Restoration, the Church releases repentant sinners from their sins [7] (based upon their confession of Christ) and restores them[8] back to the fellowship of the Church.[9]

Moreover, in instances of called men or women of God who have sinned and repented before God, the Church, according to the Biblical pattern, restores them back to their place of service and even to the potential of a higher dimension of God's call and anointing! [10]

1-(Rom. 3:23-24); 2-(1 Cor. 1:27-29; 2 Cor. 4:7; 1 Tim. 1:12-16); 3-(Eph. 4:24; Col. 3:10; 2 Cor. 5:17-20); 4-(Luke 4:18-19; 7:20-23); 5-(Jer. 15:19; 1 Cor. 6:9-11); 6-(John 3:16-17; 8:3-11); 7-(John 20:22-23); 8-(Gal. 6:1-2; James 5:19-20); 9-(1 Cor. 5:1-5; 2 Cor. 2:6-11); 10-(Luke 22:31-32; Acts 2:14; 3:1-6; 9:1, 13-16; 22:4-15).

d. Christ is waiting for the Church to complete her assignment of Restoration before He returns to the earth.

Knowing that the earthly assignment of Jesus was drawing to a close and that He had promised to return again to the earth, [1] His disciples questioned Him as to the sign of His coming and the end of the world.[2] Contrary to the common assumption of most people, He first warned them not to be deceived by false declarations, wars or even persecutions. [3] Then gave the key that unlocks the mystery of His return: *"And this gospel of the kingdom shall be preached in the whole world for a witness to all the nations, and then the end shall come"*. [4] As to when the Church would accomplish this assignment, Jesus stated that it would remain a mystery, sealed in the divine foreknowledge of only the Father Himself. [5] As with all Biblical truth, full understanding is not given in the beginning but is progressively revealed. Jesus gave further revelation to His disciples just prior to His ascension into heaven with a simple answer to their limited world-view question. [6] *"You shall receive power when the Holy Spirit has come upon you; and you shall be My witnesses both in Jerusalem, and in all Judea and Samaria, and even to the remotest part of the earth".* [7] Additional revelation is given to the Church concerning the return of Christ in Peter's Pentecostal address, when He preached that Jesus was taken up and "held" (dechomai) in heaven *until* a "restoration" (apokatastasis) of God's rule is established on earth. [8] The writer of Hebrews confirms this revelatory truth in declaring that Jesus is presently sitting at the right hand of the Father *waiting* (and will continue to wait) *until* His enemies are set under His feet.[9] It is important to recall that Jesus had previously established a foundational truth (in parable form) that His return and the fullness of His kingdom would not be as imminent, as many suppose, but would occur after He gave His servants time to accomplish an assignment. [10] The obvious Biblical implication from these scriptures is that God's Church has a divine mission to accomplish before Christ will return again. This assignment is to bring restoration (through the power of the Holy Spirit) to people, to the kingdom of the world and even to the earth itself—returning them back to the rule of God in Christ.[11]

1-(Luke 21:27; John 14:3); 2-(Matt. 24:3); 3-(Matt. 24:4-13); 4-(Matt. 24:14); 5-(Matt. 24:36; Acts 1:7); 6-(Acts 1:6-7); 7-(Acts 1:8); 8-(Acts 3:20-21); 9-(Gen. 3:15; Rom. 16:20; Heb. 10:12-13); 10-(Luke 19:11-27); 11-(Gal. 6:1-2; Rev. 11:15; Rom. 8:19-23).

X. INSTRUMENTS
OF GOD'S ONGOING GRACE

A. Of the Grace of God

The grace of God is His divine empowerment, beyond any human merit, which makes possible the salvation of fallen men and women and their further preparation for a life of service unto God. It is the power of God's prevenient grace that brings salvation to all men and His abiding grace that enables them to live a righteous life in the midst of an ungodly world. [1] Through the gift of God's grace, power is given to be witnesses for Christ and to preach the mysteries of salvation to the unbelieving world. [2] By grace, power is given to men and women of God to perform great wonders and signs in keeping with the mission of the Church in the world. [3] It is only the grace of God that can provide strength and give endurance to Christians who are suffering and being persecuted for the sake of the Gospel.[4] According to the grace ("charis") of God working in us, Christians receive powerful gifts ("charisma") for the purpose of effectively serving God and ministering to others.[5] In addition to the gift of power received from God's grace, the Christian also receives the gift of peace with God knowing that by His grace the previously hostile and estranged relationship between man and God has been reconciled.[6] Finally, the working of God's grace has not been limited to people of Biblical time periods, but God's grace is extended to all people regardless of culture and time. [7]

1-(Eph. 2:8; Rom. 1:16; Titus 2:11-14); 2-(Acts 4:33; Eph. 3:7-9); 3-(Acts 6:8); 4-(2 Cor. 12:7-10); 5-(Rom. 12:6-8; 1 Cor. 12:1-31); 6-

(Col. 1:20-22; Eph. 1:2-12; 1 Pet. 1:2-5); 7-(John. 17:20; Acts 2:39; Heb. 13:8).

B. Of Faith:

1. The Meaning and Origin of Faith:

According to the Biblical definition, Faith is the "substance" (literally: the firm foundation of confidence) of belief in God and the "evidence" (literally: the absolute proof) that there is a God whom is unseen to the natural eyes .[1] The obvious question, therefore, is where does Faith come from and how is it acquired? Knowing that the finite cannot comprehend the infinite and that sinful man can never relate to a Holy God, the only hope man has of believing (having faith) in God is by His self-revelation. [2] Consequently, Faith is not a feeling, an emotion, or an exercise of blind hope, but, simply stated, *Faith is a response to God's prior action.* [3] This "prior action" of God is the grace of His self-revelation by which He has continually appeared to men and made Himself known. [4] Throughout the ages, God has revealed Himself through supernatural appearances,[5] the evidence of His creation, [6] the sacramental power of the Holy Scriptures [7] and most especially the appearance of the Son of God Himself. [8] Therefore, man is without excuse and can never please God [9] if he deliberately ignores the conviction and testimony of the Holy Spirit [10] and fails to respond in faith to these obvious "evidences" of the existence of God and His offer of salvation. [11]

1-(Heb. 11:1); 2-(1 Chr. 28:9; Matt. 11:25-27; John 6:44); 3-(Ps. 36:9; Matt. 16:16-17; John 6:65); 4-(Titus 2:11; 3:4-5); 5-(Ex. 3:2-6); 6-(Rom. 1:19-20; Heb. 1:3); 7-(Luke 24:25-27; John 5:39;

2 Tim. 3:15); 8-(John 1:1, 14; 14:8-11; Heb. 1:1-3); 9-(Rom. 1:20; Heb. 11:6); 10-(1 John 5:7, 10); 11-(John 3:19-21).

2. The Application of Faith:

Once a person responds in Faith to the grace of God's self-revelation, he then has the opportunity to enter into the grace of salvation whereby he is justified before God; he is at peace with God, and he gains approval from God. [1] Through Faith, access is given to God and His Kingdom, and one inherits the treasures of His blessings in the heavenly realm. [2] Through Faith, the Spirit of Christ actually comes to dwell within the heart of the believer, strengthening him and enabling him to comprehend the infinite love of Christ and to be filled with the fullness of God.[3] By uniting Faith with Scripture, it becomes the living and powerful Word of God that equips one for service and enables him to enter into the works of God that were prepared before the foundation of the earth.[4] By Faith in God and His promises, believers are able to walk in the "realms of the impossible" in which all things become possible for the purpose of acting on His behalf and for the furtherance of His Kingdom on earth. [5] By applying Faith, one obtains a righteous witness for God and against evil as he obeys God,[6] denies the pleasures of sin[7] and overcomes the devil and the kingdom of the world, not loving his live unto death.[8] Faith sees beyond the natural senses and temporary setbacks of life into the eternal realm of the invisible workings of God and the mysteries of His Kingdom. [9] Faith is not self-initiated religious actions according to the dictates of the human mind, [10] but rather *faith enters into the "finished work"* of God [11] and brings the resources of heaven (the hope realm) into the reality of the earthly realm. [12] According to one's Faith, healing is received for infirmities of oneself and others. [13] Finally, when Faith is made a lifestyle and life has run its course, it is one's Faith that guarantees that he will be raised from the dead to dwell eternally with our God and Savior. [14] However, Faith is a living and growing work of God's grace. Accordingly, it must be fed by diligently seeking God and by hearing and reading the Word of God.[15] Consequently the Bible gives a very clear and sober warning that the possibility of apostasy is very real, even so much as to confirm that some will fall away from the grace of God and become "shipwrecked" in regard to their faith. [16]

1-(Rom. 5:1-2; Eph. 2:8; Heb. 11:2); 2-(Eph. 2:18; 3:12; Luke 12:32-33; Col. 2:3; Heb. 6:12); 3-(Eph. 3:16-19); 4-(Heb. 4:1-3; 5:12; Eph. 2:10; 2 Tim. 3:16-17); 5-(Mark 9:23; 11:22-24; John 15:7-8; Eph. 3:20; Col. 1:10-12); 6-(Heb. 11:4-8); 7-(Heb. 11:24-26); 8-(Heb. 11:35-38; 1 John 5:4; Rev. 12:11); 9-(2 Cor. 4:18; 5:7; Matt. 13:11); 10-(John 8:28-29; 14:10); 11-(John 19:30; Heb. 3:19; 4:1-3); 12-(Mal. 3:10; Matt. 6:10; Heb. 11:1); 13-(Mark 5:34; 10:52; Matt. 8:6-13; 15:28;); 14-(Gal. 3:11; Col. 2:12; Rom. 6:3-5); 15-(Heb. 11:6; Rom. 10:17); 16-(Luke 8:13; 1 Tim. 1:18-20; 4:1-2; Heb. 3:6-19; 6:4-6; 10:26-31).

C. Of Covenant:

Through sin and rebellion, the once harmonious relationship between God and man was broken leaving man estranged from God's presence and alienated from His purposes on earth. Covenant is an instrument of the Spirit of Grace in which God provides a "spiritual bridge" to reach and restore fallen man for His work. [1] Through Covenant, God establishes a divine **partnership** with man in order to accomplish His eternal purposes on earth and in heaven.

Covenant, according to its meaning, is a two-way agreement in which God initiates His covenant with us and we respond with our covenant back to Him. It is a "morally" binding **relationship** rather than a legal contract, and it flows from an obedient heart, and not from the law. Covenant begins with a *promise* from God followed by His set *conditions*. In order for Covenant to be effective, there must be a tangible *commitment* (or Pledge) by both parties to ratify it. When conditions are met, they become a signature or "seal" guaranteeing that the two parties will abide by the conditions of the Covenant. *Testing*, in the form of difficult personal choices, is a very necessary part of Covenant, because it reveals the sincerity of both parties to keep the conditions. Then when believers faithfully respond to God's Covenant, the *benefits of Covenant are realized* and His promises are enjoyed. Thus by keeping God's Covenant, believers share in His work, live out His will on the earth and are guided by His providential care to the extent that ultimate victory over Satan will be realized regardless of personal suffering or pain. Furthermore, Covenant becomes God's method of finding who will be His people and who will make Him their God. [2] All those who respond to God's Covenant with a willing heart of obedience become His people, and those who do not respond, will not receive the benefits of His promises. Hence, Covenant is a lifetime binding agreement between God and man. The serious nature of covenant must be realized— that God promises both rewards for diligent obedience and also punishments as consequences for disobedience. [3] Therefore, Christians must become mindful of what God expects and never become comfortable in breaking any part of the covenant. But, when anyone breaks or fails to meet the conditions of the Covenant, then it must be re-

membered that <u>God never breaks His part of the covenant</u>!⁴
Through repentance, obedience and recommitment, Covenant can be restored. ⁵

1-(Heb. 10:29); 2-(Ex. 19:4-6; 2 Chr. 16: 9); 3-(Deut. 28); 4-(Rom. 3:3; 2 Tim. 2:13); 5-(Deut. 30:1-11; 1 John 1:9).

1. The Conditions of Covenant:

The conditions of Covenant are not "works", that would earn or merit the grace of God, but are human responses to God's gracious offer of Covenant. In order for a believer to be in "Covenant" with God, the following tangible commitments must be made on the part of man:

a. Salvation:

A Covenant relationship with God cannot exist without the initial act of salvation in which the hostile relationship of fallen man toward God is reconciled and man again has access to the presence of God. ¹
Salvation is a life-long commitment of trusting in the saving grace of the Lord Jesus Christ, continuing to seek Him for the forgiveness of sins, and walking in the restored relationship of obedience and purpose in God's Kingdom. ²

1-(Col. 1:21-2); 2-(John 3:3, 5, 16; Rom. 10:9-10; Philip. 2:12-16)

b. Repentance:

An unrepentant person will never receive the benefits of God's Covenant. ¹ Repentance begins with godly sorrow, ¹ recognizing that one's life has been lived contrary to God's will and that one's actions have grieved the heart of God. True repentance must be confirmed by turning away from sin and by forsaking selfish motives through the sanctifying work of the Holy Spirit.[2] The fruit of repentance produces a life that actively seeks first the Kingdom of God and that walks toward a life of righteousness as provided through the atonement of Christ. [3]

1-(Jer. 8:5-6, 10, 13); 1-(Rom. 2:4; 2 Cor. 7:10-11); 2-(John 8:10-11; Acts 3:19; 26:20); 3-(Matt 6:33; 2 Cor. 5:21).

c. Water Baptism:

In the Old Covenant, the uncircumcised male was guilty of breaking the Covenant of God.[1] Correspondingly, in the New Covenant, the heart of the covenant believer must be spiritually "circumcised" through Water Baptism,[2] meaning that flesh attitudes are being "cut away" as he follows Christ and walks in an everlasting commitment to God. Through the sacrament of Water Baptism, the believer spiritually enters into death and burial with Christ and is raised in the newness of His resurrected life. [3] Water Baptism prepares the repentant believer to receive the gift of the Holy Spirit [4] and becomes the Christian's public entrance into the Body of Christ and into new relationships with the community of believers.[5]

1-(Gen. 17:10-14); 2-(Rom 2:28-29; Col. 2:11-12); 3-(Rom. 6:3-6); 4-(Acts 2:38); 5-(Acts 16:30-34).

d. The Lord's Supper:

Christ Himself is the Mediator of the New Covenant provided by His shed blood.[1] Unless the believer receives the mysterious presence of the body and blood of Christ in the sacrament of the Lord's Supper and acknowledges His redemptive work on his behalf, he has no Covenant of eternal life. [2] Furthermore, as often as Christians partake of the Table of the Lord, they make a proclamation on earth and in heaven of the sacrificial work of Christ and the promise of His glorious return. [3] However, because of the extreme significance of this sacrament, believers are admonished by Scripture not to partake in an unworthy manner but to be self-examining as to not be guilty of the body and blood of the Lord. [4]

1-(Heb. 9:14-15; 12:24; Eph. 1:7); 2-(John 6:53-57; Matt. 26:26-28); 3-(1 Cor. 11:26); 4-(1 Cor. 11:24-31).

e. Church Attendance:

The holy observance and celebration of the Sabbath was a perpetual Covenant and sign between God and His people signifying that He had set them apart (sanctified them) for His special purpose. [1] In keeping with this commitment of Covenant, the New Testament Church traditionally met on the first day of each week (the Lord's Day) to worship and celebrate the Table of the risen Lord. [2] Furthermore, the writer of Hebrews admonished the New Testament Christians not to forsake the assembling together as the Church (called out ones) of Christ. [3] The Church gathers together for the purpose of worshiping God, receiving the preached Word, partaking of the sacraments, and ministering and fellowshiping with other believers.[4] By regularly attending church services, believers make the Lord's Day a priority in their lives signifying the Lordship of Christ over their time. With the presence of the Holy Spirit actively working through the Five-fold/Ascension Gift ministries in the Church, Christians are matured in their faith and are further prepared for ministry to one another and to the world.[3]

1-(Ex. 31:13-17); 2-(Matt. 28:1-7; Acts 20:7; 1 Cor. 16:1-2; Rev. 1:10); 3-(Heb. 10:23-25); 4-(Acts 2:41-47); 5-(Rom. 10:17; Eph. 4:11-16).

f. Submission to Spiritual Authority:

In the sovereign design of God, He has chosen to accomplish His will and communicate the terms of His Covenant through those whom He calls to lead His people. [1] Consequently, God considers complaints and rebellion against His chosen leadership (who are charged to speak for God) as though it were personal complaints and rebellion against God Himself. [2] In the New Testament Church, God deposits spiritual eldership in men and women for the purpose of leading and guiding His Church to the maturity of Christ.[3] The Bible assures us that God will severely judge leaders who violate the trust of God or misuse their authority for personal gain. [4] True spiritual authority, however, is always Christ-like and is never oppressive or contrary to the character of God. [5] Scripture, therefore, requires believers to honor and submit to the Biblical counsel, warnings, exhortation and admonition of anointed eldership, for they watch over the souls of God's people as undershepherds of Christ.[6]

1-(Gen. 17:10-11; Ex. 3:7-10; 4:15-16; 19:3-9; Amos 3:7); 2-(Ex. 16:8-12; Num. 12:1-10; 16:41-45; 1 Sam. 8:8; Ps. 105:15); 3-(Eph. 4:11-16); 4-(Num. 20:11-12; Ezek. 34:1-10; Zech. 11:17; Heb. 13:17; James 3:1); 5-(1 Cor. 11:1; 1 Peter 5:1-4); 6-(Heb. 13:17; Ezek. 3:17-21; 1 Thess. 5:12-13).

g. Giving of Tithes and Offerings:

The giving of Tithes and Offerings not only honors God but it also honors His priesthood[1] and finances the ministry of His Church on earth. [2] Those who deliberately withhold their tithes from the Lord are in fact robbing God and, consequently, bring upon themselves a curse, for the Tithe is holy to the Lord.[3] The motivation for giving Tithes and Offerings, however, should never be out of fear, obligation or guilt. All gifts unto the Lord should be as choice "first fruits" of our labor. They are given from a heart of gratitude toward God, acknowledging His goodness and greatness as the Creator of all things, the author of all life, and the giver of all gifts. [4] In giving Tithes and Offerings to the work of the Lord, the "storehouse" of God's Church is filled with both spiritual and natural provisions to allow the Five-fold/Ascension Gift ministers and those supporting them to give their time fully to the work of the Lord. [5] Furthermore, there will be provisions available in the Church to fulfill the Great Commission of Christ and to assist the needy, for which God will abundantly reward those who sacrificially give with a cheerful heart.[6] Finally, according to Scripture and the admonition of Jesus Himself, the giving of tithes and sacrifices is most certainly required of God's people but not to the exclusion of justice and mercy and faithfulness toward others. [7] In summary, Christians are required by Scripture to: give ***Tithes*** (consistently giving ten percent of their total income as first fruits to establish God as being first in their lives); give ***Offerings*** (sacrificial giving beyond tithing to plant "seeds" in God's work that returns great blessings); and give ***Alms*** [8] (special gifts of mercy, separate from tithes and offerings, to help those who are in desperate need).

1-(Gen. 14:18-20; Heb. 7:4; 1 Tim. 5:17-18); 2(Ex. 25:1-8; Num. 5:9-10; 18:8-13, 21-24); 3-(Lev. 27:30; Mal. 3:8-9); 4-(Num. 18:8-13; Neh. 12:44; 2 Cor. 9:6-15; Ps. 116:12-19); 5-(Mal. 3:10-11; Acts 6:1-4; 1 Tim. 5:17-18); 6-(Matt 28:19-20; James 1:27; 2 Cor. 9:6-15; Luke 6:38); 7-(Matt. 23:23; Is. 58:6-7); 8-(Matt. 6:2-4; Acts 10:2-4; James 2:14-16; 1 John 3:17).

2. The Benefits of Covenant:
a. By trusting in Christ as our Lord and Savior:
There is confidence that when life is over and one's course is finished on earth, he has a Covenant guarantee of a place reserved in heaven. [1] A believer righteous before God not based upon his works but upon His work for us. [2]

1-(John 14:1-3); 2-(Rom. 5:17-19; 2 Cor. 5:21).

b. By living a life of Repentance:
Through one's Covenant with Christ, confessed sins are forgiven. [1] Even though one's conduct falls short of God's requirements, the sanctifying work of the Holy Spirit never ceases to change one day by day into the character of Christ. [2]

1-(1 John 1:9); 2-(2 Cor. 3:18; Eph. 4:22-24; Col. 3:10).

c. By being Baptized in water:

An inner spiritual change takes place in one's heart. Now "clothed" in the garment of Christ's righteousness, one's old life is replaced with His.[1] Believers also enter into a new spiritual family where old prejudices and separations are removed, and they become true brothers and sisters in Christ. [2]

1-(Gal. 2:20; 3:26); 2-(Gal. 3:28-29).

d. Every time the Lord's Supper is received:

Believers take the sacramental life of Christ within themselves and renew again the covenant in His blood. [1] Believers celebrate this "Passover" meal knowing that spiritual death has "passed over" them and they now have eternal life because of His death and resurrection. [2]

1-(Matt. 26:26-28); 2-(Ex. 12:27; Rom. 3:25; 6:22-23).

e. When believers attend church with open hearts:

They submit themselves to the dynamic of the Holy Spirit who applies the preached word to their lives, increases their faith, helps them to discover their purpose and empowers them to serve Him. [1] Church is also the place where new friends are met, Christian love is enjoyed, and many are encouraged in times of need. [2]

1-(Rom. 10:17; Acts 1:8); 2-(Col. 3:11-16; 1 Pet. 4:10).

f. By submitting to God's eldership:

Believers discover God's wisdom and solutions as they run out of answers for life's problems. Whenever one is sick or in trouble, those who watch over his soul will pray for him. [1] There is confidence that God will work all things together for one's good and that He is able to deliver one from evil. [2]

1-(Heb. 13:17; James 5:14-16); 2-(Rom. 8:28; 2 Cor. 1:8-11).

g. When believers consistently give tithes and offerings:

Believers honor God as first in their hearts and support the work of God's Church on earth. In return, He honors them with an open heaven and blesses them with even more than they can receive. [1] Moreover, His providential care will guide their lives and protect their families from the powers of evil who desire to destroy their destiny in God .[2]

1-(Mal. 3:10); 2-(Mal. 3:11; Acts 10:2-4).

D. Of Sanctification:

Sanctification (literally: holiness and separation from sin) of fallen man is grounded in the reality of God, who is Himself holy and set apart from all sin. [1] Sanctification, accordingly, is that continuous operation of God's grace by which He delivers the justified sinner from the corruption of sin [2] and renews his whole being (spirit, soul, and body) in the nature of the image of God, [3] thus enabling him to do God's will on earth. The work of God in sanctification is a Trinitarian work in which the Father is the source,[4] the Son is the agent,[5] and the Holy Spirit is the energizer [6] of sanctification. Although sanctification is initiated by the work of the Holy Spirit, it is sustained by the faith response of the believer as he yields himself to the enabling power of God's Spirit, denying evil desires of the flesh and seeking after the things of God. [7] Finally, it must be understood that the work of sanctification does not produce righteousness or "perfectionism" in the believer nor is it confined solely to external disciplines of appearances or actions (food, clothing, jewelry, cosmetics, etc). [8] It is important not to confuse sanctification with righteousness. Righteousness is an imputed condition (a spiritual position) where one is counted as righteous, not based upon any works of the flesh but fully based upon the righteousness of God and faith in His redemptive work on our behalf. [9] Sanctification, on the other hand, is a cooperative work whereby the Holy Spirit empowers the believer to be conformed in his thoughts and conduct to the character of Christ. [10] Christian conduct, therefore, is a measure of the believer's maturity in Christ as he grows in sanctification, whereas righteousness does not grow or increase, but is reckoned (regardless of the flesh) by a faith relationship with our God and Savior Jesus Christ.

1-(1 Thess. 4:3-4; 1 Pet. 1:15-16); 2-(1 Cor. 6:9-11); 3-(Rom. 8:29; Col. 3:10; 1 Thess. 5:23-24); 4-(John 10:36); 5-(Heb. 10:10); 6-(2 Thess. 2:13; 1 Pet. 1:2); 7-(Col. 3:1-11; 1 Thess. 4:1-8); 8-(Mark 7:15-23; 1 Pet. 3:3-4); 9-(Rom. 4:2-25; 2 Cor. 5:21; Philip. 3:8-9); 10-(Rom. 12:1-2; Eph. 4:17-32).

E. Of the Baptism in the Holy Spirit:

1. The Promise and Purpose of Being Baptized in the Holy Spirit:

The Holy Spirit, as the third person of the Triune God, has always been at work on planet earth even from the very beginning of time when He hovered over a chaotic and spiritually dark world bringing the creative order and Light of God. [1] The Holy Spirit transformed the lifeless earthen body of Adam into a living soul, [2] commissioned and energized Old Testament men and women of God, [3] and anointed Jesus for His earthly ministry of redemption and for the establishment of His Church.[4] God spoke through the prophet Joel that there would come a day when the Holy Spirit would be freely poured out upon all God's people. [5] John the Baptist prophetically proclaimed a Spirit Baptism, other than with water, when God's people would be baptized (literally: "immersed") in the Holy Spirit and His power (fire). [6] And the last recorded words of Jesus just before returning to heaven was a proclamation that His followers would receive power when the Holy Spirit had come upon them and that they would become His witnesses throughout all the earth. [7] Then, on the day of Pentecost, all these promises of the coming of the Holy Spirit were dramatically fulfilled. The Spirit of God filled the disciples of His newly formed Church, anointing them for their mission and gifting them for service unto God. [8]

1-(Gen. 1:2-3); 2-(Gen. 2:7); 3-(Judges 6:34; 1 Sam. 10:6-10; 2 Chr. 24:20); 4-(Matt. 3:16; Luke 4:18); 5-(Joel 2:28-29); 6-(Matt. 3:11; John 1:33); 7-(Acts 1:8); 8-(Acts 2:1-4).

2. The Necessity and Benefits of Being Baptized in the Holy Spirit:

Though nearly two thousand years have passed since that day of Pentecost, the Church of today is still in need of the gracious power and gifts of the Holy Spirit if we are to be bold and effective witnesses for Christ to our generation. [1] Even though all who are truly born again have the seal of the Holy Spirit dwelling within their hearts, [2] there nevertheless must be a personal desire for God's power and ministry gifts before the fullness of the Holy Spirit can be realized. [3] Those who earnestly seek to be baptized (immersed) in His Spirit and who yield themselves to God's purposes on earth will be filled with His power to boldly do God's work and proclaim the Kingdom of God. [4] By being baptized with the Holy Spirit, believers are gifted as leaders in the Church, [5] their natural abilities are lifted to a spiritual dimension[6] and they receive extraordinary abilities to function in the supernatural realm [7] (see "The Gifts of the Holy Spirit"). Moreover, the Baptism in the Holy Spirit becomes the catalyst in fulfilling the prayer of Jesus for the unity of all believers in His Church [8] (even to the extent of reversing the curse of the Tower of Babel). As in the day of Pentecost when people from surrounding nations (who previously had been oppressors of Israel) were brought together by the common language of the Holy Spirit, [9] so also the common experience of the Holy Spirit unifies Christians from different races and cultures. Finally, when God's people are filled with (immersed in) His Spirit, the most overriding evidence will be a consistent demonstration of love, joy, peace, patience, kindness, goodness, faithfulness, gentleness and self-control, which are the undeniable Fruit of the Spirit.[10]

1-(Acts 2:38-39); 2-(2 Cor. 1:21-22); 3-(Acts 8:14-17); 4-(Acts 19:1-8); 5-(Eph 4:8-16); 6-(Rom. 12:3-8); 7-(1 Cor. 12,13,14); 8-(John 17:20-26); 9-(Acts 2:5-11); 10-(Gal. 5:22-23).

F. Of Physical Healing :

1. The Need and Purpose for Healing:

As a result of Satan's insurrection and expulsion from heaven, chaos and spiritual darkness disrupted the once harmonious and peaceful universe. [1] Moreover, ever since Adam's sin of disobedience, the curse of sin oppresses both the earth and the entire human race with fear, suffering, futility, and physical death. [2] In addition to physiological sickness, disease and death, evil spirits torment people and inflict them with mental, emotional, and physical infirmities. [3] But God is our gracious Healer. In His infinite mercy and eternal purpose, He has decreed to reverse all that sin and the devil has corrupted and to restore His glory once again to both man and the earth. [4] Accordingly, God has set laws of healing for both the natural and supernatural realms as signs pointing to His merciful goodness and to the evidence of the Kingdom of Heaven where sin, disease, suffering and death do not exist. [5] Even the natural healing processes of the human body and the modern medical technology that alleviates suffering and extends human life are results of God's common grace as He mercifully and compassionately makes provisions for the healing of people, regardless of their spiritual condition.[6] Beyond natural healing, God makes provisions for miraculous healing as an undeniable sign of the supernatural intervention of God, dramatically demonstrating His pre-eminent power and rule over sin, sickness, demonic activity, and even physical death. [7] Furthermore, as the Creator and Sustainer of the universe, there is no limit to the types of diseases that God can heal. [8] The practical purpose for physical healing, in addition to bringing glory to God and demonstrating evidences of God's Kingdom on earth, is to extend the life of a man or woman of God in order that they may continue their purpose on earth and minister in strength and wholeness. [9]

1-(Gen. 1:2; Is. 14:12-17); 2-(Gen. 3:10-19); 3-(Matt. 17:15-18; Luke 8:27-30; 13:1); 4-(Ex. 15:26; Num. 14:21; Matt. 8:16-17); 5-(Luke 10:9; Rev. 7:16-17; 22:2-3); 6-(Matt. 5:45; Luke 6:35); 7-(Matt. 9:2-8; Mark 9:17-27; John 3:2; 9:1-33; 11:39-45); 8-(Matt. 4:23; 10:1); 9-(Matt. 8:14-15; Acts 14:19-22; 2 Tim 4:17-18).

2. Spiritual Laws of Healing:

Just as natural laws govern the physical world (laws of mathematics, gravity, motion, etc.), there are also Spiritual Laws that govern activity in the metaphysical world. Specifically as it has to do with receiving healing from the Lord, the following laws are in effect and must be obeyed if the results of healing are to be experienced:

a. Healing and the Law of Faith:

God is not obligated to provide supernatural healing outside of a personal faith relationship with Him, knowing that all things are possible for those who believe. [1] Faith is the catalyst and the channel through which God's grace of healing flows to the individual in need. God looks not only upon the faith of the person who needs healing [2] but also upon the faith of those who ask on his behalf. [3] Faith is such a powerful determining factor that even Jesus could not do many miracles in His own hometown because of their unbelief.[4]

1-(Mark 9:23; James 1:6-8); 2-(Matt. 9:22, 29; Acts 3:16); 3-(Matt. 8:5-13; Luke 5:18-26); 4-(Matt. 13:54-58).

b. Healing and the Law of Covenant:

The very first promise God gave concerning healing and protection from diseases flowed out of a covenant relationship between the Lord and His people. [1] By obeying God's commands and keeping His Covenant, a clear channel of His loving kindness is opened through which the grace of restoration and healing flows to His people. [2] Through the redemptive Covenant of the Lord Jesus Christ, He restores the soul by taking away sin and provides for the availability of divine healing to restore the body as well.[3]

1-(Ex. 15:26; 19:4-6; Deut. 7:12-15; Ps. 91:1-3); 2-(Ps. 25:10; Prov. 3:7-9; Jer. 33:6-8); 3-(Is. 53:3-5; Matt. 8:16-17; 1 Pet. 2:24).

c. Healing and the Law of Structure:

God, who is the author of order, structure and delegated authority, rules His Kingdom in righteousness, justice and love. Accordingly, He has structured His Church with leadership and protocol to reflect His righteous authority and the structure of His Kingdom on earth as it is in heaven. [1] Even in the natural structure of the family unit, God has provided a structure of headship through whom He works. [2] Those who were sick and diseased in Old Testament times came to anointed men of God to be prayed for and healed by God. [3] Likewise, in the New Testament, God has set Eldership as the shepherding structure in the Church to watch over the souls of His people and pray for those who need healing. [4] God certainly reserves the right to heal whomever He chooses even if Eldership is not available. However, structure within both the family and the Church becomes a test of obedience and a channel through which God's grace and healing flows.[5]

1-(Heb. 8:4-5; Matt. 6:10); 2-(Eph. 5:23-25; 1 Tim. 3:4-5); 3-(1 Kings 17:17-24; 2 Kings 5:1, 8-10); 4-(Heb. 13:17; James 5:14-16; Acts 3:6-9; 6:8); 5-(Ps. 133:2; Mark 9:20-27).

d. Healing and the Law of God's Higher Purposes:

The thoughts, ways and ultimate purposes of God are infinitely beyond and totally incomprehensible to the finite mind of natural man.[1] In God's eternal foreknowledge, He knows the course and final end of the lives of all men, and in the final analysis, it is God who heals and not man. [2] God, therefore, in His infinite wisdom, justice and righteousness reserves the right to heal those whom He wills according to His higher purposes, the ultimate best for the individual, and for the furtherance His Kingdom on earth. [3] The requirement that God places upon His Church is to earnestly pray with discernment, to speak words of life and hope, to fight against the works of the devil, and to encourage the faith of those who need healing and finally to trust God for the ultimate outcome. [4] In the grand scheme of God's higher purposes, physical death does not signify failure nor should it bring fear.[5] Conversely, to die without Christ is a terrifying thing and brings the consequences of eternal death and hell.[6]

1-(Deut. 29:29; Is. 55:8-9; 1 Cor. 2:14-16); 2-(2 Kings 5:6-7; Is. 43:13; 46:9-11); 3-(Ex. 33:19; Rom. 9:15-21; 11:33-36); 4-(Job 13:15; Luke 22:41-44; 2 Cor. 12:7-10); 5-(Rom. 8:36-39; 2 Tim. 4:6-8); 6-(Heb. 10:31; Rev. 21:8).

e. Healing and the Law of Gratitude and Service:
The only proper response to the grace of God's healing in the life of a believer is a grateful heart followed by a life of faithful service unto the Lord. [1] Scripture gives a stern warning that failure to respond to God with humility and gratitude for His gracious healing will lead to the loss of favor with God, even to the extent of affecting the next generation.[2]

1-(Ps. 116:1-19; Luke 8:41-43; Rom. 12:1); 2-(Deut. 8:10-20; Luke 17:12-19; 2 Chr. 32:24-26).

F. Of Deliverance:

1. The Necessity of Deliverance:
Demons, evil spirits, unclean spirits, principalities and powers, etc., are all Biblical names for spirit beings of Satan's evil kingdom who oppose God and are hostile to His people. The origin of these evil forces began with the insurrection of the archangel Lucifer (known as Satan) at which time he and "his angels" were expelled from heaven and cast to the earth. [1] Knowing that the

mission of mankind is to represent the rule of God's Kingdom and to take dominion over evil on the earth, [2] Satan deceived Adam and Eve, causing them to fall into sin and away them from God and their mission. [3] Ever since that time, fallen mankind has been ensnared by the devil, hostile toward God, and held captive to do his will. [4] With an awareness of the sins of the flesh, evil spirits enter into human lives through "open doors" of sin, [5] tormenting their minds, inflicting them with sicknesses, and in some cases, totally possessing their souls.[6] But God, in His great love and mercy toward the helplessness of humanity, decreed that He would destroy the works of the devil, reverse all that Satan and his angels had done, and deliver man from the domain and bondage of evil forces. [7]

1-(Rev. 12:3-9); 2-(Gen. 1:26-28; Ps. 8:5-8); 3-(Rom. 1:28-32; Eph. 2:1-3; Col. 1:21); 4-(2 Tim. 2:26; James 4:4); 5-(John 12:4-6; Luke 22:3; Acts 5:1-3; 1 Tim. 3:6-7); 6-(Luke 4:33-36; 8:27-30); 7-(1 John 3:8; Acts 26:18; Eph. 2:4-7).

2. Deliverance Breaks Satan's Bondage and Demonstrates God's Kingdom on Earth:

Let there be no mistake about it, the war against demonic forces is not an eccentric practice of the Christian Church, but on the contrary, it is at the very heart and core of the purposes of God, the mission of Christ, and the assignment of His Church. [1] Exercising authority over Satan and his evil forces and casting them out of the lives of people is a demonstration of God's delivering power and is clear evidence that the Kingdom of God (His rule) has come to the earth. [2] Deliverance begins in the life of a new believer at the moment of salvation when God transfers him out of the domain of darkness into the Kingdom of the Lord Jesus Christ. [3] Even though a true Christian can never be "possessed" by Satan, [4] his body, soul and spirit can certainly be attacked, oppressed and diseased by demonic forces bringing torment to his life and diminishing the effectiveness of his witness. [5] Scripture warns the Christian of demonic attack and requires us, as believers, to fervently war against and resist the devil, making certain there is no place for him in our lives. [6] Accordingly, Jesus established His Church for the purpose of overpowering the spiritual authority of evil with the command to demonstrate the works of the Kingdom of Heaven on earth.[7] To accomplish this mission, Jesus has given the Church the authority of His Name, [8] the Keys of His Kingdom,[9] the Word of God, [10] and the spiritual weapons and armor all to break the bondage of Satan and proclaim Christ's deliverance to those who are bound. [11] Furthermore, the Church must understand the subtle tenacity of demonic enslavement and so teach believers the necessity of "maintaining" their deliverance by dealing with personal sins that attract evil spirits. [12] Thus the Church, as the Body of Christ on earth, continues the works of Jesus, [13] exercises rule over evil, [14] and further prepares herself to be the "Wife" of Christ, to rule with Him when He returns. [15]

1-(Luke 4:18-19; 1 John 3:8; Gen. 1:26-28); 2-(Matt, 6:10-13; Luke 11:20-22); 3-(Col. 1:12-14; 1 Pet. 2:9); 4-(John 10:28-29; 1 Cor. 6:19); 5-(Luke 13:11-16; 1 Tim. 3:6-7); 6-(John 10:10; 2 Cor. 10:3-5; Eph. 4:22-27; 6:10-18; James 4:7-8; 1 Peter 5:8-9); 7-(Matt. 10:7-8; 16:16-18); 8-(Mark 16:17; John 14:12-14); 9-(Matt. 16:18-19); 10-(Matt. 4:4, 7, 10-11); 11-(Luke 4:18-19; 9:1-

2; 2 Cor. 10:3-6; Eph. 6:11-18); 12-(Luke 11:24-26; Eph. 4:17-32); 13-(John 14:12-13); 14-(Rom. 12:7-21; Rev. 12:11); 15-(Rom. 8:17; Rev. 5:10; 12:9-11; 19:7; 21:9-27).

H. Of Prosperity (Wealth and Riches):

Throughout the history of the Church, there have been several "pendulum swings" in its position concerning wealth and riches. One extreme refers to the House of Levi having "no inheritance", [1] Jesus' warnings of the deception of riches, [2] and Paul's admonitions to "be content" with humble means [3] as patterns for the Church to follow to avoid being entangled with the world. [4] Others, however, swing to the opposite extreme and focus the faith of the believer upon claiming all the promises in the Bible that refer to receiving the blessings of prosperity, wealth and riches because God's people are "the head and not the tail".[5] According to proper Biblical interpretation, it is important for the Church to have a balanced understanding of Scripture rather than claim one portion to the exclusion of the rest. It is God's intention to *"prosper"* His people, meaning that He will *"do good"* toward them, cause them to *"excel"* and have *"no lack"*, even to have *"an abundance"—in what ever He has called them to do*. Because most people interpret prosperity only as monetary wealth, the fullness of God's intention is lost. God certainly knows our needs even before we ask, and it is His desire to grant them as long as we "seek first His Kingdom and His righteousness". [6] And therein lies the great truth of all prosperity from God. In whatever way God chooses to prosper, financially or otherwise, it must be used to advance His cause on earth and not for personal gain or self-advancement. If God chooses to give physical wealth and riches to some, it will be for the purpose of bringing Him glory and helping those who have lack. [7] However, God may choose to prosper others in body and soul as a testimony of His goodness, for what good are riches to a sick or dying person? [8] To others God may choose to prosper with a wealth of character and a good name [9] or in great spiritual gifts to bless the Body of Christ.[10] And what riches or gifts are there in heaven or earth that can compare with the prosperity of righteousness before God and Eternal Life? [11] In conclusion, all prosperity, whatever form it may take, is from God and is to be received with gratitude and faithful service unto Him. [12]

1-(Num. 18:20-24); 2-(Matt. 6:24; 13:22); 3-(Philip. 4:11-12; 1 Tim. 3:3; 6:10); 4-(2 Tim. 2:3-4); 5-(Deut. 28:1-13); 6-(Matt. 6:8-13, 33); 7-(Deut. 8:17-18; 1 Tim. 6:17-19); 8-(Luke 12:16-21; 3 John 2); 9-(Prov. 22:1); 10-(1 Cor. 12:4-11); 11-(Matt. 16:26); 12-(Ps. 75:6-7; Col. 3:23-24).

I. Of Providence:

The providence of God, simply stated, is the administration of His sovereign plan for the universe in which He guides and directs all things toward His intended purposes.[1] God uses His angelic host, as agents of His providential work, to perform His Word and to work all things after the counsel of His will. [2] Though God is the Sovereign of the universe, His providence, nevertheless, allows for the free will of man while still working the end of all things for his good and according to the kind intention of His will.[3] God's providence controls the physical world, [4] the affairs of nations, [5] the callings and divine purposes of people's lives,[6] the provisions for human needs, [7] the limitation of temptation and sin, [8] the execution of divine judgment, [9] and the fulfillment of prayers.[10] However, as a word of warning, God's Providential Care does not foreordain people to be good or to be evil nor does it excuse them from personal accountability and obedience to God. [11] God has a universal plan for the good of all men, but He always allows human choice to be the determining factor as to those who are included in His plan and those who are not.[12] God's providence includes the following elements:

1-(Is. 43:13; 46:9-11; Rom. 8:28); 2-(Ps. 103:19-20; Eph. 1:9-11); 3-(Rom. 8:28; Eph. 1:3-9); 4-(Ps. 104:1-14; Matt. 5:45); 5-(Ps. 66:7; Acts 17:24-27); 6-(Ps. 139:16; Jer. 1:5; Gal. 1:15); 7-(Gen. 22:14; Matt. 6:25-33; Philip. 4:19); 8-(Gen. 20:6; 1 Sam. 25:26,34; 1 Cor. 10:13); 9-(2 Kings. 19:35; Acts 12:23); 10-(1 Sam. 1:10-20; Matt. 6:8; 7:7-11); 11-(Eccles. 12:13-14; Rev. 22:11-15); 12-(Is. 1:18-20; Jer. 29:11-14).

1. Provision:

God, in His infinite foreknowledge and absolute creative ability, not only knows the needs of all His creation but also makes provisions for those needs. [1] If God provides for the needs of all plants and living creatures (even insects and animals), how much more will a loving heavenly Father provide for both the natural and the spiritual needs of humankind whom He created in His very image? [2]

1-(Ps. 38:9; Matt. 6-8); 2-(Matt 6:25-34; 7:11).

2. Preservation:

Since all things were created by God and for His specific purposes, He most certainly preserves and sustains the whole of His creation holding all things together by the word of His power. [1] Moreover God, who purposefully created man in His own image, preserves His people, whom He foreknew and predestined to become conformed to the image of His Son, and protects them against harm and premature death until they have completed their purpose on earth.[2]

1-(Col. 1:16-17; Heb. 1:3); 2-(Ps 3; 91; Rom. 8:28-32; 2 Tim. 4:6-8, 17-18).

3. Direction:

God directs the plant, insect, and animal world with the imprint of patterns and instincts that cause them to fulfill the purpose for which they were created. [1] But God, having given men freedom of will yet knowing their finite wisdom, supernaturally governs the path of men, directs their lives, and points them toward His eternal purposes. [2] In a mysterious way, known only by God, He influences evil men as well as the righteous such that the end result is always good for those who humble themselves before God. [3]

1-(Gen. 1:11-12, 20-25, 29-30); 2-(Prov. 3:5-12; Ps. 37:23; Prov. 16:9; Rom. 3:28); 3-(Ex. 14:4; Prov. 16:4; 21:1; Jer. 25:9).

4. Accompaniment:

God never isolates Himself from His creation but is constantly working in, with and through it to accomplish His eternal purposes. [1] The accompaniment of the Presence of God confirms His people,[2] assures their hearts, removes all fears, [3] makes God immediately available to direct their lives, [4] and guarantees success in their assignment, because the task is impossible to accomplish without God. [5]

1-(Gen. 1:2; 2:7; Ex. 14:21-22; Mark 4:39); 2-(Ex. 33:15-16; 1 Pet. 2:9-10); 3-(Ps. 23:4; Is. 43:1-2; Heb. 13:5); 4-(Ex. 13:21; John 14:17; 16:13); 5-(Deut. 31:6-8; 1 Sam. 3:19; Mark 10:27; 16:20).

5. Second Causes in Nature and Man:

In the infinite power of God, He decrees and sets in motion the energy for natural laws with their own inherent causes and effects (gravity, momentum, storms, lightening, water, etc.). However, in the infinite wisdom of God, He reserves the right to allow these effects to occur or to <u>alter</u> them in order to bring about His higher purpose. [1] God also decrees that man, who is created in the image of God, is a free moral agent with inherent consequences or rewards related to his choices and decisions. And again, God reserves the right, in His eternal wisdom and purpose, to <u>alter the outcome</u> of man's free choices in order to bring glory to God and accomplish His higher purposes.[2]

1-(Ex. 14:25-28; 2 Kings 6:5-6; Job 1:16, 19; Luke 13:4-5); 2-(Gen. 50:20; Ex. 3:19-22; Rom. 8:28; Acts 2:23-24).

6. Timing and Coordination:

God, in the sovereign administration of His eternal purposes within His universe, coordinates and allows all subordinate powers (nature, animals, angels, and men) to act according to their natural tendencies, at the precise moment that they should, in order to produce God's higher purpose and end results. [1] Again, God never causes people to sin nor does He override their will, but, in His infinite foreknowledge, He knows the hearts of all men and allows them to respond in the freedom of their choices. [2]

1-(Gen. 22:13-14; Ex. 14:4; 1 Kings 13:21-26; Acts 5:1-15; Acts 10:17-20; 28:3-10); 2-(James 1:12-17; Heb. 4:11-13; Jer. 17:9-10; Rev. 22:11-12).

J. Of Miracles:

1. The Biblical Proof and Purpose of Miracles:

Miracles are the supernatural working of God's sovereign power transcending the natural laws of time and space in order to accomplish His providential will. Miracles may occur as cataclysmic alterations of nature, [1] supernatural healing, raising the dead, [2] or divine judgment upon the wicked,[3] but, in all cases, God performs miracles to further His cause and deliver His people from evil. [4] Angels, as agents of God's providence, are often referred to in Scripture as the instruments by which God performs miracles and accomplishes His divine purposes. [5] The Biblical record begins with the miracle of creation, [6] it ends with the miraculous resurrection of the saints and renovation of the earth, [7] and it is filled with accounts of God's supernatural power working on behalf of His people. Miracles validated the revelation of the Old Testament Prophets;[8] they authenticated the authority of Jesus as coming from God, [9] and they characterized the Apostolic ministry of the New Testament. [10] Therefore, we conclude that miracles are the "signature" of God giving undeniable proof to all those who observe, that our God is "The God" of the universe, and there is none like Him in heaven or on earth. [11] Though miracles in themselves will not bring repentance, [12] they nevertheless are "signs" capturing the attention of people and pointing beyond the supernatural event itself to the power of God and the validity of His message. [13]

1-(Ex. 14:21-22; Mark 4:39); 2-(2 Kings 4:32-35; Mark 5:22-43); 3-(Num. 16:28-33); 4-(Ex. 14:30-31; 2 Kings 6:15-20); 5-(2 Kings 19:34-36; Acts 12:21-23); 6-(Gen. 1:1); 7-(1 Cor. 15:50-52; Rev. 21:1); 8-(Ex. 14:31); 9-(John 9:15-33); 10-(Acts 3:6-10; 4:16; 9:36-42; 2 Cor. 12:12); 11-(Deut. 4:34-35; 1 Kings 18:36-39); 12-(Luke 16:27-31); 13-(John 3:2; 6:2; Acts 8:6-7).

2. Miracles in the Church of Today:

It is unfortunate, across the history of the Church, that some have questioned the existence of modern day miracles by either limiting them to the miracle of redemption or relegating miracles to an era of the past. Perhaps the problem was a weakness of faith and Apostolic authority rather than the cessation of miracles themselves! (are always limited by unbelief! [1]) There is no Scriptural evidence suggesting that signs, wonders, Apostolic authority and miracles have ceased or will cease in the Church. But, on the contrary, the Bible confirms that the gift of the Apostle and the Prophet has been permanently given to the Church [2] and that signs will follow believers to confirm the preached word. [3] Though it may not be widely recorded or publicly acclaimed, historical documents and personal testimony have proven that the miracle working power of God still operates through today's Church where there is faith to believe and the authority to perform miracles. As a final conclusion, there appears to be a very specific and definite correlation between the working of true miracles and the revelation, anointing and authority of God's Church. Powerful signs and wonders flowed through the early Church as a result of their revelation of Christ, the empowerment of the Holy Spirit and their boldness to act upon the authority that Jesus had given. [4] We are convinced that as the Church of today genuinely exercises the authority given through the commission of Christ [5], receives the power of the Baptism in the Holy Spirit,[6] and proclaims the revelation of the Kingdom of God, She will once again move in the miraculous. Then the world will receive signs and miracles as witnesses of the Kingdom of God and will experience a "foretaste" of God's rule on earth.[7]

1-(Matt. 13:58); 2-(Eph. 4:7-11; 1 Cor. 12:28); 3-(Mark 16:17-20; Heb. 2:4); 4-(Luke 9:1-2; Acts 6:8; 14:3); 5-(Matt. 28:18-20); 6-(Acts. 1:8); 7-(Luke 10:8-11; 11:20).

K. Of Perseverance of the Saints:

Though the "Perseverance of the Saints" is a generally unfamiliar doctrine to most Christians, it holds a very broad and powerful truth concerning yet another dimension of God's grace that He lovingly extends to His people. Perseverance is the work of divine grace whereby the great Triune God continues to bring to completion that which He began in the heart of each believer. [1] Perseverance has to do with God's supernatural power causing the Christian to persist in the faith, [2] endure temptation [3] and successfully complete his divinely assigned course. [4] In other words, perseverance is God's provision to help each person fulfill his/her purpose on earth, resist the work of the devil and be effective witnesses of the Kingdom of God. As with all other aspects of the Christian Faith, the variable of human choice is a determining factor in releasing God's grace and power in the individual. God provides the power of supernatural perseverance and makes it available to every believer but he must receive it and appropriate it in his life in order for it to be fully effective. Accordingly, believers must be fervent in their spirits, deny sinful desires of the flesh, and resist the devil by not giving him any opportunity to cause failure in the midst of trials, tribulations and persecution. [5] Believers must not allow themselves to compromise the character of Christ within, but rather they must flee from all temptations and diligently pursue righteousness. [6] Believers must persevere by keeping the commandments of God and maintaining their faith in Jesus even while all others are falling away. [7] Then after having done all that is known to resist evil and maintain a Christian walk, believers have confidence that by yielding to the sustaining power of the Holy Spirit, He will add the supernatural working of His perseverance to empower them to endure to the end. [8] Finally, at the end of life's journey, the ultimate reward for loving God and persevering as a faithful witness of the Kingdom of God is a guaranteed entrance into the eternal Kingdom of the blessed Lord and Savior Jesus Christ to receive a glorious crown of life in heaven. [9]

1-(Philip. 1:6); 2-(1 Tim. 1:18-19; 6:12); 3-(John 17:15; 1 Cor. 10:13); 4-(Acts 13:25; 2 Tim. 4:7); 5-(Rom. 12:11-14; Eph. 4:22-32; James 4:7-8); 6-(1 Tim. 6:10-11; 2 Tim. 2:22); 7-(Rev. 14:9-13); 8-(Matt. 10:22; Eph. 6:10-18); 9-(2 Pet. 1:6-11; James 1:12).

L. Of Progressive Revelation:

1. The Bible is the Unchangeable Revelation of God
The Bible is the written revelation of God given through inspired men of God who were moved upon by the Holy Spirit. [1] The written canon of Scripture (Old and New

Testaments) is the very Word of God and, accordingly, is the all-sufficient, infallible rule of faith and conduct for guiding people to salvation, worship and Christian service.[2] Revelation, therefore, is God's self-disclosure[3] concerning His Person, His will, His eternal purposes, and the intention of His heart toward all people and the whole of creation. Since God revealed Himself to and through the culture in which the Bible was written, proper exegetical interpretation requires a comprehensive study of Scripture[4] (context, cultures, customs, political and economic situations, and the particular "dramas" that were unfolding in people's lives) in order to fully understand God's intentions. By studying metaphors,[5] parables, [6] symbols, [7] types, shadows and patterns [8] in Scripture, we discover God's unchangeable truth in "Principle" form, which transcends time and culture and applies to all generations even to those who are not yet born.[9]

1-(2 Pet. 1:20-21); 2-(2 Tim. 3:15-17); 3-(Jer. 29:12-13; Rev. 3:20); 4-(2 Tim. 2:15); 5-(Ps. 18:2; Prov. 18:10; 1 Cor. 10:1-4); 6-(Judges 9:7-15; Matt. 13:31-52); 7-(Heb. 9:8-14; 1 Cor. 11:10); 8-(Ex. 25:40; Heb 8:5; 10:1; Col. 2:16-17); 9-(Ps. 102:18; John 17:20; Acts 2:39; Eph. 3:3-5).

2. God Progressively Reveals Himself and His Purposes to Each Generation

Knowing that each generation has its own cultural, sociological, and national issues that differ from the times in which the Bible was written, God continues to reveal Himself and His purposes to His Church concerning these present-day needs and issues. (For example, the Bible does not specifically speak to current issues such as: public housing, the lottery, state sponsored education, modern medical technology, abortions, terminating life support, artificial insemination, cloning, ecology, pollution, or reaching a generation born into broken homes and raised on television and music videos.) Therefore, God does not cease to speak to His Church, even after the writing of the Bible, but continues to give His solutions to the human needs of today. Jesus confirmed that the Holy Spirit, who was the Agent of inspiration for the Bible, would continue to <u>guide people into all truth and reveal what is to come</u>. [1] Accordingly, God has placed Apostles and Prophets in the Church of today to hear the fresh voice of God speaking into present day issues. [2] Furthermore, the Holy Spirit gifts men and women of God with the "Word of Wisdom, Word of Knowledge, and Prophesy" specifically for the work of speaking God's heart and mind to the Church. [3] And the Apostle Paul prayed that God would give the Church "<u>a spirit of wisdom and of revelation</u> in the knowledge of Him" and that the "eyes of their hearts may be enlightened" in order to know the purpose of their calling. [4] Progressive Revelation, therefore, is certainly not "extra-biblical" revelation, since it flows from Scripture and never violates nor contradicts the written revelation of God's Word but complements it with relevance. Neither does Progressive Revelation "add to" Scripture but is subordinate to the Bible, acting as an extension of the "trajectory" of God's Word and reaching to every person regardless of time, nationality or culture. Progressive Revelation, as an instrument of God's grace, is special enlightenment and fresh insight given by the Holy

Spirit to understand Scripture in light of God's will and purposes for each generation.

1-(John 16:12-15); 2-(I Cor. 12:28; Eph. 4:11-16); 3-(1 Cor. 12:4-11); 4-(Eph. 1:17-18).

XI. THE KINGDOM OF GOD AND WORLD VIEW

A. Of God's Intention for the World:

"The earth is the Lord's, and all it contains, the world, and those who dwell in it". [1] It was God who created it and structured it according to the wisdom of His order and purpose. [2] God created all things with the imprint of His divine structure as can be clearly seen in the seasonal cycles of nature, [3] the growth processes of plants, [4] the instincts of animals, [5] but most especially in the wondrous creation of man. [6] God structured the angelic host as well with divine assignments in the invisible realm of heaven. [7] God made man as the apex of His creation, breathed into him the very image and likeness (spiritual character and nature) of God, and placed him on planet earth with a heavenly mission to represent the rule of God. [8] With this awesome God-given authority, Adam and Eve were commissioned to multiply, develop family structure, fill the earth, and build structured civilizations and governments that would reflect the divine order of heaven, thus honoring God, giving glory to His name, and existing for His pleasure. [9] God's intention, therefore, is that His world would be a universal community reflecting His own creativity and productivity in an environment of health, peace and harmony forever (see "Creation").

1-(Ps. 24:1); 2-(Prov. 8:22-31); 3-(Gen. 8:22); 4-(Gen. 1:11-12); 5-(Job 39:1-30); 6-(Ps. 8:4-5; 139:13-16); 7-(Gen. 2:1; Job 38:7; Is. 6:2-3; Luke 1:19); 8-(Ps. 8:5-8); 9-(Gen. 1:26-28; 4:17; Rev. 4:11).

B. Of the Kingdom of the World (World Systems)

The insurrection and expulsion of Satan from heaven cata-strophically disrupted God's divine order and purpose for His creation and brought chaos, disorder, and deception to the earth. [1] Satan especially targeted Adam and Eve, as the representatives of God's Kingdom, and ensnared them in his kingdom of rebellion, sin and death. [2] Ever since that time, the earth has been subjected to futility, and the whole world has been under the power of the evil one. [3] Conse-quently, man's creativity has been perverted into evil scheming; [4] his productivity has changed into futility, [5] and man is now enslaved to hostility, discord, fear, suffer-ing, sickness and eventual death. [6] The world now oper-ates under Satan's wicked system of self-desire, self-grati-tude, and self-exaltation. [7] Selfish greed robbed people of their righteousness; [8] personal power and gain overthrew genuine compassion and concern for others, [9] and the love of money usurped the love of God. [10] As men developed cities, nations, governments, commerce, industries and businesses within societies, their personal bent toward sin emerged and overtook every facet of civilization, even to the point of corrupting organized religion. [11] In short, all of mankind has followed after the pattern of Satan and exchanged the glory of God's rule for the corruption of his own rule apart from God. [12]

1-(Gen. 1:2; Rev. 12:3-4, 7-9); 2-(Gen. 3:1-13; Rom. 5:12); 3-(Rom. 8:19-22; 1 John 5:19); 4-(Gen. 6:5; Micah 2:1-2); 5-(Gen. 3:17-19; 4:12; Is. 14:12-17); 6-(Gen. 3:15-19; Deut. 28:20-45); 7-(1 John 2:15-17); 8-(2 Pet. 2:14-15); 9-(Jer. 22:13-17); 10-(1 Tim. 6:10; Matt. 6:24); 11-(Jer. 6:13; Matt. 23:13-36); 12-(Rom. 1:21-25, 28-32).

C. Of the Kingdom of God and Its Influence Over the World:

1. The Kingdom of God:

The Kingdom of God, in its simplest definition, is the ever-present reality of the eternal rule of God in every sphere of existence in the universe. The Kingdom of God (the government of God's rule) existed before time began; it exists now and will forever exist after time has ceased. The Kingdom of God is not limited to a heavenly realm, a geographic place, a race of people, a nation on earth, or even the Church herself. The Kingdom of God can be simplistically seen in the following elements:

a. God:

God is the Father and Creator of all things, and He rules over all His creation. [1] God rules His Kingdom, not by outward disciplines, but in righteousness, peace and joy. [2] All people who submit their lives to the rule of God will bear the seed of righteousness and yield the fruit of His Holy Spirit. [3]

1-(1 Chr. 16:25-34; Ps. 66:1-7); 2-(Ps. 99:1-5; Rom. 14:17); 3-(Gal. 5:22-23; James 3:17-18).

b. The King of God's Kingdom:

The King of God's Kingdom is Jesus Christ whom God installed by virtue of His Son's creative and redemptive work. [1] Jesus is the Son of God, expressing through human flesh the exact representation of the nature of the very person of God. [2] There is salvation in no other name than Jesus, and no one can enter the Kingdom except through Christ the King.[3] Many know Jesus as Savior, but few yield to Him as the Lord and King. [4]

1-(Ps. 2:1-12; John 1:1-4; 1 Tim. 1:12-17); 2-(Heb. 1:2-6); 3-(Acts 4:10-12; Matt. 25:31-34); 4-(John 1:49; Luke 6:46; 2 Pet. 1:11).

c. The Subjects of the Kingdom:

These are the ones who are born into His Kingdom by the Holy Spirit, [1] delivered from the domain of darkness, and transferred into the Kingdom of God's Son. [2] They obey the King from their heart and not out of fear or constraint.[3] Not all who join a church or who even speak of exploits in God's name are His subjects but only those who obey Him as the King Eternal.[4]

1-(John 3:3-8); 2-(Col. 1:13); 3-(Rom. 6:16-18; 2 Cor. 9:7); 4-(Matt. 7:21-23).

d. The Laws of the Kingdom:

The Laws of the Kingdom are matters of faith, righteous character and godliness [1] written internally on the hearts of God's subjects [2] and expressed externally as described in the Sermon on the Mount. [3] Keeping the laws of the Kingdom is not a matter of outward disciplines of any religious system but of yielding to the indwelling Spirit of God who produces obedience from the heart. [4]

1-(1 Tim. 4:7-8; 6:11; 2 Pet. 1:3-11); 2-(2 Cor. 3:2-3; Heb. 8:10); 3-(Matt. 5, 6, 7); 4-(Rom. 2:25-29; John 16:13-15; 1 Pet. 1:2-3).

2. The Church is Called to Model the Kingdom of God as a Witness to the World:

From the very beginning, man was created in the image and likeness of God and placed on a hostile planet to rule in God's stead, to guard against evil, and to represent His Kingdom of righteousness. [1] Though mankind failed in his mission, God raised up His Church, calling man out of the darkness of Satan's domain and empowering him with His Holy Spirit for the very purpose of warring against evil and fulfilling his original assignment as God's witness on the earth. [2] Having redeemed man from sin, Jesus returned to heaven and gave to His Church the responsibility of governing His Kingdom on earth until He comes again. [3] Thus the sons of the Kingdom (the Church) are the "seeds" of the Kingdom of God planted in the soil of the world to grow and influence it for God.[4] The Church is the "Embassy" of the government of God strategically placed in the kingdom of the world to bear witness to God's Kingdom. [5] The assignment of the Church is to "model" (demonstrate) the character, compassion, order, structure and, will of God's Kingdom on earth as it is in heaven. [6] The Church is God's active human agency on earth charged with a dual mission. First, the Church is to preach salvation in Christ [7] (at which the traditional church is very proficient). Second, the Church is to model the Kingdom as a witness and influence to the world [8] (about which the traditional church knows very little). Once the Gospel of the Kingdom has been preached and demonstrated as an adequate witness, then God will have a proven standard working through His Church by which He will judge the nations of the earth. [9]

1-(Gen. 1:26-28; Ps. 8:4-9); 2-(Matt. 16:18-19; 1 Pet. 2:9-10; Acts 1:8); 3-(Luke 12:32; 19:11-27; 22:29-30); 4-(Matt. 13:33, 37-43); 5-(2 Cor. 5:19-20); 6-(Matt. 6:10; Philip. 2:13-16); 7-(1 Cor. 1:17-24); 8-(Matt. 5:14-16; 10:7-8); 9-(Ezek. 16:51-52; Matt. 11:20-24; 24:14; 1 Cor. 6:2).

3. The Strategies of the Kingdom to Reach (Influence) the World:

Jesus, through the means of a parable, made the astonishing observation that "the sons of this age are more shrewd in relation to their own kind than the sons of light". [1] Unfortunately, many churches have misinterpreted scriptures that deal with separation from the world and have developed monastic attitudes that have become counterproductive to reaching the world for Christ. Jesus, when sending His disciples into the world, instructed them to be "shrewd as serpents, and innocent as doves". [2] Thus, the Church must discover and take advantage of the methods of the world to effectively reach people while maintaining their purity of purpose and the character of Christ. God is very concerned about the bondage Satan has over the nations of the world otherwise He would not have directed His Church to "make disciples of all nations". [3] Hence, the Church must have strategies as to how to communicate to the world and correctly represent Christ and His Kingdom. The Church must know how to address pertinent issues within every kingdom of the world in order to influence them for Christ. Without the proper God-given strategies, the earth, which is under the power of Satan's evil system, will never be reclaimed for God.

1-(Luke 16:8); 2-(Matt. 10:16); 3-(Matt. 28:19).

a. The Strategy of Love and Compassion:

Love is the divine motivation and foundation for all Christian ministries. Love is always self-giving and never self-seeking, desiring the good of another even at the expense of one's own desires and agenda. [1] Love that is unconditional is redemptive, being at the very heart and core of God's vicarious sacrifice of His own Son .[2] Love never exposes sin to others, but quietly brings God's solution for sin and restores one back to his place of service. [3] Love never condemns those who have been ensnared in sin but compassionately brings forgiveness, removes shame, and leads people into the freedom of a new life in Christ.[4] Love does not seek to "lord" over others but leads by serving others just as Christ came to serve us. [5] And of course, the Lord Jesus Christ is our example to follow, since He is the epitome of God's Love working in a real human being .[6] When the Church receives a "Baptism of Love", the world will see the witness of God's love working within the Church, and all people will know that we are the followers of Christ. [7] Moreover, when the people of the world experience genuine Christ-like love, expressed by the Church, then they will know that the influence of the Kingdom of God has come their way. The strategy of Love and Compassion will never fail to accurately represent and bring a witness of the Kingdom of God on earth.[8]

1-(1 Cor. 13:1-13); 2-(John 3:16); 3-(1 Pet. 4:8; Gal. 6:1-2); 4-(John 3:17; 8:11; Rom. 8:1); 5-(Matt. 20:25-28); 6-(John 13:14-15; Heb. 1:3); 7-(John 13:34-35); 8-(Matt. 9:35-36; 1 Cor. 13:8, 13).

b. The Strategy of Relating to the World:

The strategy of "Building Relationships" is one of the most obvious yet one of the Church's greatest stumbling blocks to reaching the world. The Bible makes a very simplistic observation that two men cannot walk together unless there is agreement. [1] Unfortunately, many Christians are fearful of "walking with" the world lest they be seen by others and counted as being "bound with unbelievers" or having "friendship" with the world.[2] This has led to wholesale exclusion of the world by many churches and indiscriminate condemnation of sinners requiring that they "get saved" before any relationships can be developed. God most certainly warns believers never to enter into "covenants" with the unbelieving world or to partake in deeds of darkness,[3] however, unless Christians are able to identify with people from all walks of life and all moral conditions, the world will never be reached. Jesus, once again, is our example of how God compassionately reaches out and even befriends those considered social and religious outcasts in order to bring salvation to their lives. [4] The Apostle Paul, in describing his zeal to win the lost, avowed to become all things to all men, that he may by all means save some. [5] In today's society, this translates into relevant methods of relating to the world, which may include the use of secular music sounds with Christian lyrics, the use of drama and dance in public worship, and the use of television and the internet. In addition, the Church may sponsor coffeehouses and homeless centers in the inner city, develop support groups for the addicted and for those of other lifestyles, and offer singles clubs for those not married or divorced. The Church must learn that in the final analysis, the world is not our enemy, but on the contrary, *the world is our field of service!* Hurting people are looking for friends, and unless the Church is willing to become their friend, the world will never be introduced to the true character of God and His Kingdom.

1-(Amos 3:3); 2-(1 Cor. 6:14-17; James 4:4); 3-(Ex. 34:11-16; 1 Kings 11:1-2; Eph. 5:3-10); 4-(Matt. 9:9-13; Luke 7:34-50; 15:1-32; 19:1-10); 5-(1 Cor. 9:19-22).

c. The Strategy of Influencing Leadership:

God is the ultimate authority in the universe and His Kingdom is a government of divine rule and order. According to the pattern of His Kingdom, God established a structured world with order, design and governing authorities in every facet of civilization. [1] God set headship in the family as the basic unit of society to maintain order and to direct each family according to the will of God. [2] God set kings and governmental rulers over nations for the orderly administration of society. God set legal systems in place for maintaining law, order, justice and fairness for the people. Even commerce and private businesses are administered by principles of structure and delegated authority. And finally, God set governing structures in His Church to hear from God, to equip His people, and to facilitate the ministry of the Church on earth.[3] Since all authority begins with God, is accountable to God, and ends with God, it would behoove all human authorities to bow in submission to the rule of God and to His great power.[4] By wisely using this pre-set plan of God's structured world, the Church produces far-reaching results and multiplies her productivity by purposefully influencing leadership groups in society. When the Church influences heads of families, heads of businesses, heads of legal systems, and heads of states, then she will effectively reach family members, industrial workers, lawmakers, and ultimately the nations. [5] When the Church awakens to the call of God to be the "conscience" of government and society, then she will begin to fulfill the great commission of Christ to disciple nations, bring them into covenant, and teach them to obey God.[6] As a final word of warning, however, the Church must be keenly aware that the devil also understands the power of influence. [7] He knows that by gaining control over governing authorities in society, he also gains control over society; and by targeting visible leaders in the Church, he destroys the credibility of the Church's witness to the world. [8] Therefore, the Church must be aware of the schemes of the devil and be ready to war against Satan's influence wherever it may occur. [9]

1-(Rom. 13:1-7; 1 Pet. 2:13-20); 2-(Gen. 18:19; Eph. 5:22-31; Col. 3:18-21); 3-(Ex. 18:15-23; Eph. 4:16-17; 1 Tim. 3:1-5); 4-(Ps. 2:1-12); 5-(Gen. 41:14-16, 39-44; Dan. 2:16-20, 46-49; Esther 7:1-10; 8:1-17); 6-(Matt. 28:18-20); 7-(Matt. 16:11-12; Mark. 8:15; 1 Cor. 5:6-8); 8-(Job 1:8-11; Zech 3:1-3; Luke 22:31; John 10:10; Luke 4:1-13); 9-(Eph. 6:10-19; 1 Pet. 5:89).

---

d. The Strategy of Giving Real Solutions for Human Problems:

The world is not looking for shallow cliches, religious jargon or emotional hype but rather real answers and real solutions to problems that plague society. Hurting, sinful and guilty people don't need the condemning finger of the Church, but they do need forgiveness, acceptance and hope in the midst of their hopeless situations. [1] If the Church is going to model the Kingdom of God, she must not shy away from addressing the social issues of the community that oppress and hold people in bondage. [2] God's Church must become His instrument for social change that increases the quality of life, helps people to reach their potential in God, and leads them to their purpose in living. Where society has fallen into sin and degradation, the Church must restore people back to human dignity and show them how their lives can be renewed according to the image of the Creator. [3] Where people are trapped in poverty and illiteracy, the Church must feed, educate and help them find employment. [4] Where the sick, widowed and elderly are alone, afraid, and dying, God's Church must bring healing, comfort and hope. [5] Human governments may have many beneficial social programs to help people, but only God's Church has permanent solutions for the problems of sin that befall the unfortunate. And in some cases when governments are ignoring the cries of hurting people, the Church must step in as the moral conscience of society to protect the rights of the oppressed and give them a voice to bring about reform. [6] Even when it comes to the abuse of the earth and the waste of natural resources that sustain life for on-coming generations, the Church, as God's custodian over the earth, must influence governments and initiate changes to protect the earth from destruction.[7] When the world runs out of answers for the problems of society and sees workable solutions that genuinely change the course of human lives coming from the Church, then there will be a credible witness that the Kingdom of God has influenced the world.

1-(John 8:11; Rom. 8:1); 2-(Luke 4:18-19); 3-(Jer. 15:19; Col. 3:8-17); 4-(Matt. 25:34-40); 5-(Lev. 19:32; 2 Cor. 1:3-4; James 1:27; 1 Cor. 15:19); 6-(Ex. 3:9-10; Prov. 22:22-23); 7-(Gen. 2:15; Rev. 11:18).

4. The Kingdom of God is the Ultimate Kingdom:

Since the rule of God always was, always is, and always shall be infinite and eternal, it becomes an obvious conclusion that His Kingdom is the ultimate Kingdom and all lesser kingdoms, whether angelic or human, will ultimately bow to God and His Son. [1] God is the Sovereign of the Universe who removes and establishes kings and His dominion is from generation to generation. [2] Though the Systems of the World may rage against the authority of God and His Son, [3] the Kingdom of God, which will never be shaken or destroyed, will crush all other kingdoms and put an end to all authorities who rise against God's righteous rule. [4] God has sovereignly set His Church as the "seed" of His Ultimate Kingdom planted in the field of the world. [5] Though it may have begun as the smallest of earthly institutions, she will continually grow, as leaven, until she becomes a great refuge for the nations and covers the earth with the knowledge and glory of the Lord. [6] Then when the secular falls apart, the sacred will step in, and Christ will rule the nations and govern His Kingdom along with the Church, His Bride. [7]

1-(Rev. 1:8; Rom. 14:11; Philip. 2:10-11); 2-(Ps. 103:19; Dan. 2:21; 4:3); 3-(Ps. 2:1-3; Rev. 11:18; 19:19); 4-(Ps. 2:4-12; Dan. 2:44; Heb. 12:28-29); 5-(Matt. 13:37-43; John 17:15-20); 6-(Matt. 13:31-33; Is. 11:9-10; Hab. 2:14); 7-(Is. 9:6-7; Rev. 2:26; 5:9-10; 15:3-4).

XII. THE CONSUMMATION OF ALL THINGS

Just as God began His marvelous drama with the creation of the heavens and the earth, so God will also bring all things to a fitting conclusion in accordance with His eternal purposes and decrees. Thus, God's *Authority* will continue to be pre-eminent; His *Visible Creation* will have served its purpose and be transformed into the glorious abode for Him and His people, and His *People* will forever be His Bride and heirs of the Kingdom. Through *Freedom of Choice,* God will bring every creature, whether angelic or human, into a place of *Accountability* to Him, and through His *Covenant,* God will have made a way for the salvation and restoration of all people who receive Him as Lord and Savior. And finally, God will bring *Correction and Restoration* to His universe by destroying all that is evil and restoring all things back to the order and control of His eternal kingdom and to the glory of His righteous rule. (See "The Eternal Purposes and Plan of God for Heaven and Earth.)

A. Of the End of Physical Life for Each Individual:
1. Physical Death:
Physical death is the direct consequence of the curse of sin that Adam and Eve brought upon the entire human race through their disobedience to God.[1] Physical death results from "Spiritual Death" (separation from God) and is the termination of physical life by the separation of the spirit/soul from the body.[2] Physical death, in addition to being God's chastisement for sin, also serves to humble the proud and bring to an end the oppressive dominion of unrighteous and wicked men. Though all

human beings, both good and wicked, are under the curse of death, [3] beyond physical life and death is the eternal realm of life and death. Eternal death is that ultimate and irrevocable final estate of the wicked that are eternally separated from God having refused to receive His gracious plan of redemption. [4] But for those whose righteousness is in Christ, though they die physically, they have passed out of spiritual death into spiritual life and will never taste of eternal death.[5]

1-(Gen. 2:16-17; Rom. 5:12; 6:23); 2-(Gen. 35:18; Eccles. 12:7; James 2:26); 3-(Eccles. 9:2-3); 4-(2 Thess. 1:8-9; Rev. 20:6; 21:8); 5-(John 5:24; 1 Thess. 4:16; Rev. 2:11).

2. The Immortality of the Soul:

Man is the only creation of God made in His own image and likeness and into whom He personally breathed His Spirit. [1] Accordingly, God has set eternity in man's heart causing the soul of man to be immortal, living forever even beyond the grave.[2] Scripture never speaks of death as annihilation or non-existence (even of the wicked) but of eternal consciousness and awareness.[3] The continuation of God's eternal purposes for man and his personal accountability to God would have little meaning if there were hope in this life only.[4]

1-(Gen. 1:26-27; 2:7; Ps. 8:5); 2-(Eccles. 3:11; Matt. 10:28); 3-(Mark 9:43-48; Luke 16:22-31); 4-(1 Cor. 15:19).

3. The Interval Between Death and the Resurrection:

According to Scripture, immediately upon physical death, the spirit/soul of every human being is judged and transported into the eternal realm, [1] either into confinement, torture and eternal separation from God [2] or to be in the eternal presence of God beholding His light and glory. [3] In addition, there is an impassable "chasm" that spiritually separates those in heaven from those in hell and prohibits any contact of people on earth with the dead.[4] Any attempt to do so on the part of human beings is forbidden by God since it opens human souls to the entrance and control of evil spirits. [5] The Bible never refers to an alternative "holding place" for the purification of the dead nor does it imply that the dead abide in some "neutral existence" waiting for the resurrection. For the wicked, life immediately after death is a conscious state of eternal pain, suffering, weeping, anguish, and even regret for those who will share their end. [6] But for those who are righteous in Christ, they will be truly alive even after death, made perfect in holiness, and forever in eternal rest and bliss. [7] At the resurrection, however, each will stand before the judgment seat of God to receive the final judgment and return again to either heaven or hell with bodies that will never die![8]

1-(Heb. 9:27); 2-(Luke 16:19-31); 3-(2 Cor. 5:8; Philip. 1:23; Luke 23:42-43); 4-(Luke 16:23-31); 5-(Deut. 18:10-12; 1 Sam. 28:7-19; 1 Chr. 10:13); 6-(Matt. 13:41-42, 49-50; Luke 16:23-28; 12:47-48); 7-(Luke 16:22-23; Rev. 7:13-17; 14:13; 21:3-5); 8-(Mark 9:43-48; Rev. 20:11-15).

B. Of the Return of Christ:

1. The Second Coming of Christ:
According to Scripture and the personal testimony of the Lord Jesus Christ Himself, He will return person-

ally [1] not just figuratively, to the earth. His return will be a physical return in bodily form [2] as differentiated from the "spiritual enlightenment" of the indwelling of the Holy Spirit. Christ will visibly return for every eye to behold Him and not as some "secret appearance" to a select few. [3] When Jesus returns, it will be a sudden, one-time cataclysmic event, totally unexpected to the unbelieving world, but anticipated and expected by those who know the times, seasons and signs that lead to His return. [4] And finally, the return of Christ will be glorious and triumphant as He appears as the King of kings and Lord of lords with the clouds of heaven, accompanied by the holy angels and the armies of heaven which are His saints. [5]

1-(John 14:3; Acts 1:11; 1 Thess. 4:16); 2-(Acts 3:20-21; Heb. 9:28; Rev. 1:7); 3-(Acts 1:11; Matt, 24:23-30; Col. 3:4; Tit. 2:13); 4-(Matt. 24:32-51; 25:1-13; Tit. 2:13; Rev. 22:11); 5-(Matt. 24:30; 1 Thess. 3:13; 4:16; 2 Thess. 1:7, 10; Rev. 19:11-16).

2. The Role of the Church and the Signs of His Coming:

The obvious question that people desire to ask in relation to the end of the world is when Jesus will return and bring the fullness of His Kingdom to the earth. Even the disciples of Jesus asked this same question with their limited Israel-centric world-view, and their assumption that at the end of all things God would bring the kingdom to Israel. Jesus answered, without responding to the shallowness of their question, by telling them that what they really needed was the power of the Holy Spirit to be His witnesses, not just in Jerusalem but also throughout all the earth as well. [1] Herein lies a great revelation concerning the understanding of the return of Christ and the end of the world. Without being baptized with the Holy Spirit, there is no prophetic understanding [2] of the events surrounding the Second Coming and no power to fulfill the commission of Christ to witness of Him and His Kingdom throughout the earth.[3] Though no man, except the Father, knows the day or the hour of the return of Christ and the end of the world,[4] with the power of the Holy Spirit the Church can prophetically discern the season when all things are ready and prepared for His coming.[5] Thus the Church will not be mislead with rumors of wars, weather events, or some outward signs thinking that His return is imminent. [6] Since Christ is the Head (in the midst of His Church) [7] and the Church dwells in the light of the Holy Spirit's revelation and truth, the Second Coming of Christ will not overtake us as a harmful thief in the night. [8] Furthermore, since God's Church is His "key player" in preaching the Gospel of the Kingdom as a witness to the world, she will not be caught off guard when the end is at hand. [9]

1-(Acts 1:5-8); 2-(John 16:12-15); 3-(Matt. 24:14; Acts 4:33); 4-(Matt. 24:36); 5-(Matt. 16:1-4; 24:32-34); 6-(Matt. 24:3-8; Luke 17:20-21); 7-(Luke 17:21; Rev. 1:12-13); 8-(1 Thess. 5:1-11): 9-(Matt. 24:14).

a. Christ will return when the Church completes her Assignment:

Jesus spoke incredibly profound and prophetic truths in the simple parables of life. Such was the case in the parable He told to those who supposed that the Kingdom of God would appear immediately. Jesus clearly illustrated that while the "nobleman" was away waiting to receive his kingdom, he left his servants behind to "do business" and "increase his holdings".[1] Likewise, Jesus left His Church on earth to complete "His business" and "increase His influence" on earth until He returns. Scripture clearly teaches that heaven must receive (lit: "holds by necessity") Jesus <u>until</u> restoration is complete on earth. [2] In addition, we learn that when Jesus returned to heaven, He "sat down at the right hand of God, <u>waiting</u> from that time onward <u>until</u> His enemies be made a footstool for His feet". [3] Who else, but the Church, has been commissioned to war against the enemies of God, [4] prevail against the authority of hell, [5] and overcome Satan by crushing him under her feet through the power of the Holy Spirit? [6] Who else, but the Church, has the Keys of the Kingdom to release people who are bound by Satan's grasp and bring restoration to those who are trapped by sin? [7] Jesus made it abundantly clear that the end would not come until His Church preaches and witnesses (demonstration in Spirit and power, not just persuasive words [8]) the Gospel of the Kingdom (the rule of Christ) to all the nations who are entrapped in world systems. [9] (See Kingdom of God and World View.)

1-(Luke 19:11-27); 2-(Acts. 3:21); 3-(Heb. 10:12-13); 4-(2 Cor. 10:3-6); 5-(Matt. 16:18); 6-(Rev. 12:11; Rom. 16:20); 7-(Matt. 16:19; Luke 4:18-19; Gal. 6:1-2); 8-(1 Cor. 2:4); 9-(Matt. 24:14).

b. Christ will return when the Church is Mature:
Upon the completion of His redemptive work on be-

half of fallen men, Jesus structured His fledging Church with the Five-fold/Ascension Gift Ministries for the purpose of leading His Church into maturity.[1] Jesus used the imagery of a seed of grain in order to relate the concept of maturity to the natural mind. [2] Just as a crop must be mature for there to be a harvest, so the Church must be brought to the fullness of her ministry as seeds sown in the world before souls can be harvested out of the nations into the Kingdom of God. [3] Without maturity, the Church can not have the "mind of Christ" or understand the hidden mysteries of the Kingdom [4] nor will she have the spiritual discernment to be aware of the subtle schemes of the devil. [5] Without maturity, the Church will never come into unity, and consequently jealousy and fighting will destroy her witness to the world. [6] Without maturity, the Church will not have the compassion nor the anointing to restore people held captive by the evils of society and their own sins. [7] Only through the power of the Holy Spirit working through the Five-fold/Ascension Gift Ministries can the Church grow up, prepare herself and become the mature Bride of Christ.[8] When Christ returns, He will be returning for a Church who has matured in her character and mission and is ready to be glorified with Him as co-ruler of the Kingdom of God. [9]

1-(Eph. 4:8-16); 2-(Mark 4:26-29); 3-(Ps. 106:45-47; Is. 11:9-12; Matt. 13:37-43; Mark 13:27; Rev. 14:15); 4-(1 Cor. 2:6-16; Luke 8:10); 5-(Heb. 5:14; 1 Cor. 12:10; 2 Cor. 2:11); 6-(John 17:21-23; 1 Cor. 3:9; Gal. 5:15; James 3:16); 7-(Luke 4:18-19); 8-(Eph. 4:14-16; Rev. 19:7; 21:2); 9-(Rev. 21:9-11; 22:5).

c. Christic will return when World Systems fail and the Church has God's Solutions:

All the nations of the earth are on a collision course with destruction, because they have partaken in the deception of the devil and have chosen to make for themselves a name and a build their own kingdom apart from the rule of God. [1] These are the people who have given themselves over to the god of world systems and who have partaken of the "spirit of the antichrist", denying Christ as the Son of God and the Ruler of His Kingdom. [2] Just as with the Tower of Babel, God will bring utter confusion among their ranks, and they will end up destroying themselves as did the wicked nations who fought against God's people. [3] The world will continue to grow wicked and further indulge in Satan's world system of atheism, lawlessness and mammon, but the Church, through the power of the Holy Spirit, will increase in maturity, authority and revelation from God. [4] Finally in the fullness of time and according to the eternal purposes of God, Babylon (World Systems), whose king is Satan himself and whose inhabitants are all the demonic forces of evil, will fall and be overthrown by the judgment of almighty God.[5] But also according to the providential working of God's infinite wisdom, the sons of the Kingdom, who have been planted within the World Systems, [6] will shine as the sun with answers and solutions that are beyond the wisdom of the world. [7] And then when the Church has accomplished her faithful witness on earth, there will be great rejoicing in heaven such as the world has never known, and Christ will return for the marriage supper with His Bride and the saints will be glorified with Him forever.[8]

1-(Gen. 11:3-4; Ps. 2:1-3; Is. 14:14; Rev. 12:9); 2-(2 Cor. 4:3-4; 1 John 2:18, 22; 4:3); 3-(Gen. 11:5-9; Judges 7:22; Is. 19:2-4); 4-(2 Thess. 2:3-4; Matt. 24:10-14); 5-(Is. 13:19-22; Rev. 14:8; 16:19; 17:5-6; 18:2-24); 6-(1 Pet. 5:13); 7-(Matt. 13:37-43; Philip, 2:15-16; Gen. 41:14-16, 39-44; Dan. 2:16-20, 46-49); 8-(Rev. 19:1-21).

3. The Purpose of Christ's Return:

The return of Christ to the earth has nothing to do with natural Israel but has everything to do with His Church and the final conclusion to the earthly drama of His Kingdom. Natural Israel has the same opportunity as all other nations of the earth to accept Christ as their Lord and Savior and become a part of His Kingdom. If Israel is to be saved, they must be grafted into the New Covenant in Christ in order to be accepted by God and again become "the Chosen People of God" along with all who have been saved by His grace. (See "The Church as Spiritual Israel".)

a. Christ is returning to consummate the Final Redemption of all Believers:

Redemption, as discussed previously, is a continual process whereby the repentant sinner receives the saving grace of God in Christ and begins a life-long journey of being changed by the power of the Holy Spirit from glory to glory into the image and character of Christ. [1] The final conclusion of a life lived to the glory of God and in submission to His rule is the reward of a redeemed body, glorified and transformed from sin and corruption by the resurrecting power of the Holy Spirit. [2] As one of the most amazing and final works of God's grace and mercy, all the saints in heaven and those still alive on earth at His coming are allowed to partake in the glorification of Christ by being glorified with Him.[3] And thus the Bride of Christ will be His Wife in eternity, glorious, brilliant, honored, and chosen before the foundations of the world as heirs and co-rulers of the Kingdom of God.[4]

1-(Rom. 8:29; 2 Cor. 3:18; Col. 3:10); 2-(1 Cor. 15:50-55); 3-(Rom. 8:17; 1 Thess. 1:10; 4:15-17); 4-(Rev. 21:9-27; 22:5; Eph. 1:4-6).

b. Christ is returning to utterly destroy all that is evil and usher in His Eternal Kingdom of Righteousness:

As a final conclusion of God's eternal purpose to correct and restore a rebellious universe, God will exercise the full weight of His judgment and wrath upon all wickedness in that "Terrible Day of the Lord". [1] God is infinite in His love, grace and mercy but equally infinite in His holiness, justice and righteousness. (See "The Character of God".) God's mercy and grace are seen in His redemptive acts on behalf of guilty sinners,[2] yet for those who belligerently and maliciously refuse the grace of salvation and continue in self-willed rebellion, God unleashes eternal judgment and retribution. [3] Since the total understanding of the method of destruction is beyond human comprehension, the Biblical imagery suggests that God Himself will personally destroy all that is evil. [4] Then when all evil has been removed from the earth, only Christ's righteous Kingdom will remain.[5]

1-(Is. 13:6-13; Mal. 4:5-6; 1 Thess. 5:2-3); 2-(Is. 1:18-19; Rom. 5:6-10); 3-(Ex. 34:7; Is. 1:20; 2 Pet. 2:9-10; 3:7-12); 4-(2 Thess. 1:6-9; 2:8; Rev 19:11-21); 5-(2 Pet. 3:13; Rev. 21:1, 26-27; 22:3).

C. Of Tribulation and the Millennium:

1. Tribulation:

Throughout church history, there have been many variations of theological interpretations concerning the concept of Tribulation (Lit: intense affliction, distress, and persecution). Some have attempted to view it as the unique and unparalleled judgment of God upon the world lasting for a set duration of time to which the church may or may not be subject. Though God will undoubtedly release the full weight of His judgment upon all wickedness (and never upon His Church for whom He died), the term "tribulation" is almost always used in the scriptural context of affliction and persecution from a corrupt world under the evil influence of satanic forces. We conclude, therefore, that ***Tribulation is satanic persecution and attack upon God's people*** [1] resulting from man's mission to exercise the rule of God's Kingdom over evil on the earth. [2] Though man has always been under tribulation and persecution, [3] Satan has increased his persecution as a result of the increased anointing upon God's Church due to the outpouring of the Holy Spirit. [4] When Scripture speaks of "great tribulation", it is pointing toward Satan's ever increasing attack upon the Church that will continue to grow, because he knows his time is growing short. [5] God, however, in His infinite wisdom and power, even reverses the evil results of Satan's persecution by using it to press God's people to persevere against evil, proclaim Christ with great zeal and to enter fully into the Kingdom of God in spite of all obstacles of the devil. [6]

1-(Matt. 13:21; John 16:33; Rev. 2:9-10); 2-(Gen. 1:26-28; Matt. 24:9; Rev. 1:9); 3-(Deut. 30:7; Ps. 119:85-87; Jer. 17:18); 4-(Acts 8:1-4); 5-(Rev. 12:12); 6-(Acts 8:4-5; 14:22; Rom. 5:3-5; 12:12; 1 Thess. 1:6).

2. The Millennium:

The early church wrestled with trying to understand the concept from Revelation chapter 20 of a "thousand year" binding of Satan and reign of Christ with a subsequent releasing and then final destruction of Satan. Many attempted to interpret this passage as a "literal" 1,000 years, and some, in recent history, have even tried to force National Israel into the equation as a "Theocratic kingdom of the Jews". By properly understanding the metaphoric use of numbers in Scripture which give deeper meaning to spiritual concepts, the number "1,000" denotes "**absolute and complete**" [1] victory of Christ over Satan. We conclude, therefore, that Revelation 20:1-10 speaks to the *entire Christian Era*, which is a *present reality* rather than a future event! The Christian Church is ruling (with Christ) *now* as a kingdom of priests with the victorious Christ as the Head of the Church and the King of His Kingdom. [2] The "binding of Satan" has already taken place in the spiritual realm with Christ's victory over the devil [3] and will continue to take place in the earthly realm as long as the Church exercises her authority over the power of Satan and uses the Keys of the Kingdom. [4] The evil power of Satan, however, is very much alive and he continues to thwart, attack and persecute the Church and take viscous advantage of every opportunity to capitalize on human sin.[5] But in fullness of time, the eternal judgment of God will most certainly bring a final destruction to Satan himself, including all that are actively engaged in his wicked system. [6]

1-(Deut. 32:30; Ps. 50:10; 2 Pet. 3:8; Rev. 20:2); 2-(Rom. 8:37; 1 Cor. 15:57; Rev. 1:5-6); 3-(Eph. 4:8; Col. 2:15; Heb. 2:14; Rev. 1:18); 4-(Matt. 16:19; Luke 9:1-2; 10:19); 5-(2 Cor. 2:11; 1 Thess. 2:18; 1 Pet. 5:8); 6-(Rev. 19:20; 20:10).

D. Of the Resurrection of the Dead:

1. Resurrection of both the Righteous and the Wicked:

Both the Old and the New Testaments speak directly to the reality of a physical resurrection of the dead (for both the righteous and the wicked) at the end of time. [1] The resurrection of the dead is most certainly a mystery[2] to the natural mind and can only be accepted by faith in the truth of God's Word. In this great mystery of the end time, resurrection is the work of all three persons of the Triune God, [3] completing the believer's redemption by spiritually glorifying the physical human form and making it free of the corruption of sin and earthly imperfections. [4] As inconceivable as it may seem, not only will the righteous receive bodies that will never die, but the Bible clearly teaches that the wicked will as well. [5] While the righteous are resurrected to the glories of eternal bliss in heaven, the wicked are raised for the purpose of receiving the total judgment and justice due for a life of wickedness and rebellion against the rule of God. [6] Finally, concerning the time of the resurrection, proper understanding of Scripture clearly indicates that there is only one resurrection which includes the righteous and the wicked at the end of the world, coinciding with the Second Coming of Christ and immediately preceding the final judgment. [7] (The Rev. 20:6 reference to a first resurrection pertains to the New Birth and not a bodily resurrection.)

1-(Is. 26:19; Dan. 12:2; John 5:25-29; Acts 24:15); 2-(1 Cor. 15:51); 3-(2 Cor. 1:9; John 5:21-29; Rom. 8:11); 4-(Rom. 8:22-23; 1 Cor. 15:35-55; Philip. 3:20-21); 5-(John 5:28-29; Acts 24:15; Rev. 20:13-15); 6-(Rom. 1:32); 7-(John 5:21-29; 6:39-40; 1 Thess. 4:16; 2 Thess. 1:7-10).

2. The "Transformation" of those who are alive (the issue of the "Rapture"):

Much controversy in the Church has arisen concerning the full understanding of the "catching away" ("harpazo") of the saints who are still living on earth and their "transformation" into glorified bodies at the Second Coming. This is unfortunate, since the intention of this passage was to "comfort" those who believed that the saints who had previously died would be at a disadvantage. [1] It is also unfortunate that erroneous doctrines have been developed which foster an "escapism" mentality within the Church. This promotes Christian irresponsibility by causing some to passively wait for Jesus to "rapture" His Church out of the world and the troubles of life. The truth of Scripture requires God's

Church to boldly represent the Rule of God on earth, war against evil and the work of Satan, and demonstrate a credible witness to the world by responsible Christian living. [2] This Scripture is meant to confirm that both the living and the dead in Christ will be included in the great end time redemption and glorification of the bodies of the saints by being "changed (lit: 'transformed') in a moment, in the twinkling of an eye" .[3]

1-(1 Thess. 4:13-18); 2-(Ps. 8:5-6; 2 Cor. 10:3-6; Rom. 5:3-5; Col. 4:5-6); 3-(1 Cor. 15:51-52).

E. Of the Final Judgment and Final Estate (Heavenand Hell):

This is the finality of personal accountability to God. According to Scripture, God requires all His moral creatures, both human and angelic, to appear before His judgment seat at the end of the world. [1] In the grand scheme of God's eternal plan, it is most fitting that Christ Himself, the King of His Kingdom [2] and the Incarnate Mediator between God and fallen men,[3] should be the Great Judge of the Universe to determine the eternal estate of all His creatures.[4] **Heaven** is that eternal abode of God Himself,[5] where all the radiant goodness and glory of His presence [6] is freely and forever available to the Redeemed of the Lord who have loved His appearing.[7] **Hell,** on the other hand, is the realm of eternal separation, spiritual darkness, defilement, torment and anguish. It is reserved for the devil, his angels and all fallen men and women who refuse the gracious offer of redemption and follow in the pattern of Satan's pride and rebellion.[8]

1-(Eccles. 12:13-14; Rom. 14:11-12; Rev. 20:11-15); 2-(Matt. 25:31-34); 3-(John 5:26-27; Acts 10:40-42; 1 Tim. 2:3-6); 4-(Rev. 1:12-18; 20:11-15); 5-(Matt. 6:9; Rev. 4:1-11); 6-(Ex. 33:18-23; 34:5-8); 7-(Rev. 7:9-17; 2 Tim. 4:7-8); 8-(Luke 16:23-31; Matt. 13:41-42; 22:13-14; Mark 9:43-48).

1. The Judgment of the Devil and his Angels:

The most obvious and first recipients of God's final judgment and eternal confinement into everlasting hell are the devil (who sinned from the beginning) [1] and the angels who followed his pattern of insurrection. [2] In the infinite wisdom and justice of God, He judges Satan and his demonic forces by the witness of the Redeemed of the Lord who were once held captive by the devil but have been delivered out of his domain into the Kingdom of Christ. [3] In this final act of God's judgment over Satan, He brings into reality the decree made in the Garden of Eden to crush the head of Satan and fulfills the purpose of the Church's faithful witness against evil throughout all the ages past. [4] According to the Word of God, the devil and his angels will be "thrown into the lake of fire and brimstone, and they will be tormented day and night forever and ever". [5]

1-(Matt. 25:41; 1 John 3:8); 2-(Rev. 12:3-9; 14:9-10; 19:20; 2 Pet. 2:4; Jude 6); 3-(1 Cor. 6:3; Eph. 5:8; Col. 1:13); 4-(Gen. 1:26-28; 3:15; Job 1:6-22; Eph. 3:9-11; Rev. 12:11); 5-(Rev. 20:10).

2. The Judgment of the Wicked:

The concept of people (especially friends or family members) experiencing a punishment of never-ending pain, suffering and anguish in eternal hell with no hope whatsoever of relief or reprieve is more than any compassionate person can handle. The obvious question is how can a loving and compassionate God impose such an ultimate and tragic fate upon people whom He created in His own image? The answer lies in both the character of God and in the freedom of human decision. Though God is infinite in His love and mercy, He is also equally infinite in His holiness and righteousness. Through God's love for fallen men, He made a way of escape from the spiritual death of Adam's race and at unimaginable costs satisfied the demands of His holiness in the Substitutionary Atonement. By giving mankind freedom of choice, God offers the only way of escape [1] allowing men to freely choose to accept Christ or walk away from salvation. [2] Therefore, man has no excuse because the light of Christ has reached to every man and His law is written in every heart,[3] even to the evidences of God in His creation.[4] Thus, man judges himself by walking away from the light of God [5] and brings upon himself the demands of eternal condemnation of sin and unrighteousness. Consequently, unrepentant men fully deserve and will most certainly receive the punishment of eternal hell.[6] Nevertheless, God is also infinitely just in His judgments and will only punish the wicked according to the degree of their wicked deeds. [7]

1-(Acts 4:12); 2-(Mark 10:21-23); 3-(John 1:9; Rom. 2:14-16); 4-(Rom. 1:18-20); 5-(John 3:19-21); 6-(Matt. 13:41-42; 25:41-46; Rev. 20:15; 21:8); 7-(Luke 12:46-48).

3. The Judgment of the Righteous:

Many have felt that those who have had their sins forgiven and have received the righteousness of Christ will not have to be subject to the judgment.[1] While this is true in respect to a judgment of condemnation and hell, the Bible clearly teaches that even the righteous will undergo a <u>type</u> of judgment as well. [2] Again, in the absolute justice of God, He allows the good to stand with the wicked to emphasize the saving grace of God and bring glory to Christ who bought fallen souls and redeemed them with His blood. [3] Since all have sinned, neither the saint nor the sinner deserve heaven, yet the saint will be publicly judged "Righteous and Forgiven" based upon their redemption in Christ [4] and all their works of unrighteousness will be "burned up"! [5] But for the unrepentant sinner, who refused salvation in this life, he will be condemned and judged as unrighteous and worthy of eternal hell. Then, in the presence of all, the righteous in Christ will be welcomed into the glories of heaven [6] wherein lies the River and Tree of Life with eternal joy, gladness, peace and rest. [7] Here the redeemed believer will receive his rewards for faithful service unto the Lord [8] and will enter into the fullness of the presence of God as His Wife and Co-ruler of His Kingdom forever. [9]

1-(John 5:24); 2-(Eccles. 12:14; Rom. 2:6-8; 14:10); 3-(Rev. 5:9-10); 4-(Rom. 3:23-26); 5-(1 Cor. 3:10-15); 6-(Matt. 25:21-30); 7-(Rev. 14:13; 21:3-7; 22:1-5); 8-(Matt. 5:11-12; 10:41-42; Luke 6:35-36; 1 Cor. 3:8; Rev. 22:12); 9-(Rev. 5:10; 22:5).

F. Of the Renovation of the Earth:

Few people truly understand the great value that God places

upon the earth in the grand scheme of His plan.[1] The physical creation has served its purpose well as God's time/space "stage" where He unfolds His eternal purposes and the "drama" of His plan. As a final fulfillment of God's eternal purposes for the earth and all creation, He will set it free from the corruption of sin and satanic influence that has caused groaning and suffering.[2] With the Final Judgment and removal of all wickedness, God will not destroy the earth, but will <u>purge</u> the heavens and the earth of all unrighteousness and <u>renovate</u> it for the final abode of glorified humanity.[3] The earth will again become that "Garden of the Lord" without hostility or sin where the righteous dwell in total security and spiritual rest with God.[4] And finally, upon this renovated and renewed earth, God and His people will reign together in His Kingdom forever.[5]

1-(1 Chr. 29:11; Ps. 24:1-2); 2-(Ps. 98:7-9; Rom. 8:19-22); 3-(Ps. 102:25-26; 2 Pet. 3:12-13); 4-(Is. 11:6-10; 51:3-6; 65:25; Rev. 21:3-4; 22:3-4); 5-(Is. 60:21; Rev. 22:5).

G. Of the Fulfillment of the Kingdom of God:

1. At long last, the great "Drama" of the universe is complete:

The final chapter of the great panoramic drama of God's eternal purposes in heaven and earth will close with total wisdom, justice and victory. The Kingdom of God that was once disrupted by rebellion and sin will be fully restored to order, obedience and righteousness. All evil will be removed and all things will, in eternal reality, be fully restored[1] just as God had spoken through the prophets of old, the Apostles of the New Testament, and the

Son of God Himself. God will continue to righteously rule in His universe, yet even with a new dimension of glory, for there will be a "New Song" sung in heaven of the marvelous grace of God who redeemed and made victorious His Church to rule with Him in heaven forever![2]

1-(Acts 3:21; Heb. 10:13); 2-(Rev. 4:11; 5:9-10).

2. The Final Sequence of Events:

As in a gloriously choreographed coronation of an earthly king receiving his kingdom before all his subjects (and even his enemies), so there will be a great heavenly sequence of events finalizing the wondrous drama of God, His King, and His redeemed people.

a. The victorious *Christ will return* in all His splendor and glory to regain His Kingdom that was won by His Church whom He redeemed and empowered.

b. There will be the wondrous *resurrection of the dead,* both good and evil, to prepare for the great and *Final Judgment* of God over His creation.

c. All evil and wickedness will be judged, removed and destroyed from the universe by the victorious Christ Himself.

d. God's Son, as the eternally installed *King, will deliver His Kingdom (that He* regained from

the power of the evil one) back to the Father
to whom it rightfully belongs.
(1 Cor. 15:23-24)

e. *The glorified saints will inherit the Kingdom*, prepared for them from the foundations
of the world, and will reign with God in the new
heaven and earth forever and ever.
(Matt. 25:34)

3. The Final Reality of the Kingdom of God:

All the promises and partial evidences of the Kingdom
of God that were received and embraced on earth by the
Church will, in fact, be an eternal reality. God will no
longer be "in heaven" and man "on earth", but His im-
mediate presence will be forever with man in total fulfillment of relationship. God's Church will no longer
yearn for the anointing of God, but His people will be a
radiant people adorned for her Husband—cleansed, pu-
rified and glorified in splendor. God's people will no
longer have to seek after revelation of God and His truth,
but the full Light and Glory of God will fill all the earth.
Then the prayer Jesus taught His disciples to pray, "Thy
Kingdom come, Thy will be done on earth as it is in
heaven" will be a reality forever and ever. Amen!

PRINCIPLES OF INTERPRETATION

(Reprinted by permission from *The Ultimate Kingdom*)

An approach to study scripture by the Spirit supersedes natural methods, and this is difficult for the natural mind to comprehend. Where are we today in the Church and in reestablishing God's Kingdom and authority on this earth? Before we can learn the answer to this much-asked question, we must learn the principles of interpretation. There are seven principles of interpreting the Word of God, which is interesting because seven is the number of completion or perfection.

Principle number one: The Word of God was written by the Holy Spirit and can be understood only under the inspiration of the Holy Spirit. Many attempt to make the Bible a book of science or poetry. While it is true that prose and poetry are contained in the Word, it was not written as taught in many colleges and universities to be just a book of literature. The Bible was written by "holy men of old, as they were moved upon by the Holy Spirit." While the hand of man was used by the Holy Spirit to write the Scriptures, only the Holy Spirit fully understands and can impart what He said to us. Man's natural mind does not know. In II Timothy 3:16 we read:

> *All scripture is given by inspiration of God, and is profitable for doctrine, for reproof, for correction, for instruction in righteousness: that the man of God may be perfect, thoroughly furnished unto all good works.*

Principle Number Two: The Word of God was written to reveal man's final and total victory in Jesus Christ. The Bible was not written to prove that the sons of Adam and Eve went to another country to find wives, yet through the years people have argued about that and many other things found in God's Word. Why, in truth, was the Word written? The beloved disciple, John said, "And many other signs truly did Jesus in the presence of His disciples, which are not written in this book ... (John 20:30). What book was John speaking of? The Bible, the Word of God.

Principle number three: God has something special to say in each book of the Bible. As we study, it is important that we find the core or message of each book. Genesis, for example, is the book of beginnings. If there is revelation, it must have a point of origin, so we have to find out why we're here. In Genesis we learn that man was created to be the pleasure of God. We learn also how man got into trouble, and we catch a glimpse of how he's going to get out of trouble, which is more fully explained by other chapters of the Bible. All the blood relationships, which are documented, are nice to know from a historical viewpoint, but they have little to do with the overall thrust of the book. What God was saying was, "I put man in a garden because I wanted to have fellowship with him. He was made in My own likeness, and I gave him a choice, a will to choose good or evil. This makes man a god. But he fell ... he blew it." Genesis 3:15 tells us that the offspring of the woman shall bruise the serpent's head. There is the first promise of redemption, and that's what Genesis is all about-a promise of restoration.

God has something special to say in each book of the Bible. When the books are put together, they compile what the Holy

Spirit believes mankind must have at their disposal to use as instruments to accomplish God's purposes.

Principle number four: Determine by the Holy Spirit to whom God is speaking or communicating. In the gospels it is apparent that God is communicating to the whole world: "For God so loved the world" (John 3:16). In Hebrews the Holy Spirit is addressing the Jews, because He says, "You had one covenant, but I will show you a better covenant." He said that in prior times, God has spoken to us by the prophets, but in these last days, He has spoken to us by His son, Jesus Christ. The whole book of Hebrews is addressed to Christian Hebrews who had not yet learned that they had entered into a new covenant relationship.

Paul's Corinthian letters illustrate this principle very well. According to historical facts, there were approximately thirty to forty thousand Christians at Corinth when Paul wrote to them. Although they did not all assemble at the same place, there was only one church, not several individual churches. The Corinthian Christians had many shepherds, but when the Apostle Paul came, he was their authority.

The Christians held fellowship meetings with their shepherds at various sites around Corinth, but on the occasions when the whole church came together, people came from all over the city. Some rode up in their big chariots bringing fine wine and sumptuous food, and they assembled in their own little groups to eat, drink and fellowship. Others from poorer communities sometimes didn't even have enough food to feed their people. Those with the abundance of food and wine gorged themselves and became drunk while the other group went hungry. When Paul learned what was happening, he reprimanded the people.

"What? Have ye not houses to eat and to drink in? Or despise ye the Church of God, and shame them that have not?" In most churches today, this drunken revelry is not a problem as it was in Corinth, so there is no point in trying to apply Paul's admonishment to ourselves when the circumstances don't fit. We must know to whom and in what circumstances God is speaking.

Principle number five: What is the frame of reference? First of all, what is the location? If the setting is Rome, it will have a totally different flavor than if the setting is Ephesus. What are the circumstances? In Revelation the Christians were persecuted. In some churches the people were affluent, and sometimes they had problems. In the church at Corinth there were times when it was difficult to tell the men from the women. Because of this Paul asked, "Doesn't nature teach you certain things? A woman should look like a woman, and a man should look like a man." Because of this advice which was specifically addressed to a circumstance and problem in the church at Corinth, some churches exist today, which have built almost a whole doctrine around a woman's appearance. How sad!

What are the symbols? Number symbols like seven and ten always mean perfection. In the Word of God the word mountain often symbolizes kingdom. When John spoke about a mountain in Revelation, the Jews knew immediately what he meant. I have a sneaking suspicion that the Jews knew what Jesus meant when He said, "Speak to this mountain (kingdom), and it shall be removed." Concepts of symbols, which have seemed so difficult, can be simple when we allow the Holy Spirit to give us understanding.

Principle number six: Never interpret the Scripture to prove a doctrine, system or method, but ultimately to find the purpose or goal of that revelation or scriptural teaching. Jesus clearly said, "You teach for doctrine the traditions of men." Some denominations have been built around a certain doctrine or tradition. For example, differences in concepts of water baptism have caused much dissension in the Church, but modes and methods of baptism were not important to Jesus. What God really was saying was, "I'm going to make a covenant with man, and baptism is the beginning of your discipleship." If you were in a desert without water, God would not require you to be immersed in water. Strict adherence to the letter of the law at any cost kills, but the Holy Spirit makes alive. Today it is a sad fact that at least ninety percent of the interpretation of the Scriptures is by the letter of the law and not by the Spirit. That is the reason that churches die.

Principle number seven: Remain open to additional revelation and understanding. Previous revelation points us in a direction which will not vary but will be made more beautiful and more perfect in our understanding as God reveals more of His plan to us. In these last days God, by His Spirit, is bringing us revelations we did not have previously. In I Corinthians 2:7 Paul said, "But we speak the wisdom of God in a mystery, even the hidden wisdom, which God ordained before the world unto our glory."

Wouldn't it be a sad thing to tell a child in the first grade, "Today we're going to study trigonometry?" The teacher must begin instead by saying, "If you had one apple and I had one apple, and we put those apples together, how many apples would we have?" God reveals to us only that with which He can trust us, and He reveals to us what we need to know in and for our day or generation.

Paul, on the other hand, had such a high level of revelation that God had to show him how to maintain equilibrium with his natural mind. Some people place such an emphasis on spiritual revelation that they are "of no earthly good." God can only trust us to the level of our ability to respond in the Spirit and to live out the revelation He gives. Why would He give us principles at a higher level when we cannot even handle the revelation we have? Paul understood that when he wrote to the Hebrews (5:12), "I want to go on and give some hidden manna, but I have to take you back to the very first principles over and over again. I'd like to leave those, but since you don't seem to understand them, I can't give you any more revelation."

Conclusion: If God is going to trust the Church with the revelation of the Kingdom of God, it will require mature Christians and Spirit-filled people. If we don't respond, He will take the opportunity to respond away, and that is why our responsiveness is absolutely necessary. The principle of the Kingdom is, "I'll trust you with a few things. If you show yourself responsible for them, I will give you more." Our principle is, "God, give me responsibility, and I'll show you I can be faithful." Never! God says, "Be faithful in small things and I'll give you greater responsibilities." God never, absolutely never, breaks that principle.

In Jesus's parable of the talents, one man received five talents and another only one. Whatever talent was given was the potential. Most of us are still at the level of one talent, and instead of handling that one with faithfulness, we complain because we didn't receive two or five talents, so God takes that one talent away from us. That's the Kingdom principle.

Paul said, "I've had revelations that make me free! I am free to do things that the law says I may not do. I'll be careful not to offend you by my revelation. That which the Holy Spirit has given me liberty to do, I can't give to you because you don't have the revelation or maturity." Some people want freedom without revelation, but it just won't happen. "But," Paul said, "because I'm still living in this dimension, I will be very careful not to offend you by the liberties that God has given me" (Romans 14).

Because these are the days just before the coming of Christ, Satan will spare no effort to deceive even the very elect. The demands that will be put upon us will also require new insight and new revelation, and because of the attendant persecution, a new level of unity will also be demanded. The revelations God trusts us with will help us to meet these new demands as Satan comes against us with tactics never used before to try to steal the revelation away. We're beginning to see these pressures now on levels such as in homes, in relationships, and in subtle ways in disobedience to God. The Bible says that the Kingdom message will bring a sword to divide, but we must be able to discern what is of God and what is of the devil.

The Holy Spirit will give new revelation and new insight to motivate us for God's purposes, and God will try us to see if we are sensitive to His Spirit. For that reason, God will give an increased measure of authority to the Church in these last days, because He knows we need His authority to counter the authority of Satan.

These seven principles of interpretation, which will remain steadfast, may be applied to God's Word, and the Holy Spirit will lead you into the revelation you need for these days.

Bishop Earl Paulk. *Ultimate Kingdom.* Atlanta, GA: Dickenson Press, Reprinted 1999.

Index

Spirit, 38-39; baptism in the Holy spirit, 117-119; other
related topics, 1, 2, 92, 134-137

I

Immortality 154
Incarnation 29, 30
Infant Baptism 68
Influence 43, 96-98, 141, 144, 147, 148
Intercession 33
Interval Between Death and the Resurrection 154, 155
Israel as God's people 46-49

J

Jesus Christ: His person and nature, 29; His mission and work as
King of God's Kingdom, 29-30; His mission and work as
Redeemer, 30-31; His resurrection, post resurrection minis-
try, and exaltation, 32-33; His return to the earth, 33-34, 155-
163, 172
Judgment: of the devil and his angels, 168; of the wicked, 168,
169; of the righteous, 170; other related topics 98, 172
Justice 8
Justification 23

K

Keys of the Kingdom 51, 93, 94, 125, 158, 165
Kingdom of God: God's intention for the world, 139-140; its
influence over the world, 141-151; the fulfillment of the
kingdom of God, 171-173; other related topics, 29-30
Kingdom of Satan 18, 26, 27, 30, 31, 96, 97, 123
Kingdom of the World (World Systems) 98, 140

L

Laws of healing 120-123
Laying on of Hands 72, 74
Leadership 50-65, 73-74, 90, 147-148

Tribulation 163-164
Trinity 7, 23, 29, 35, 117, 165
Truth 8, 82

U

Unity 49, 54, 74, 89, 95, 97, 118, 159

W

Water Baptism 67-68, 71, 88, 109, 114
Woman 19, 60-65
Women in Ministry and Leadership 60-65
Word of God 1, 2, 36, 85, 99, 105, 127, 136
World Systems 140, 150, 158, 160
World View: God's intention for the world, 139; the kingdom of
     the world, 140; the kingdom of God and its influence over
     the world, 141-151; the church as the model of the kingdom
     and witness to the world, 143-144; the kingdom of God as
     the ultimate kingdom, 150-151
Worship 59, 84

NOTES

NOTES